IRISH IDEAS

KENNIKAT PRESS SCHOLARLY REPRINTS

Ralph Adams Brown, Senior Editor

Series In

IRISH HISTORY AND CULTURE

Under the General Editorial Supervision of

Gilbert A. Cahill

Professor of History, State University of New York

IRISH IDEAS

BY

WILLIAM O'BRIEN, M.P.

KENNIKAT PRESS
Port Washington, N. Y./London

IRISH IDEAS

First published in 1893
Reissued in 1970 by Kennikat Press
Library of Congress Catalog Card No: 79-102620
SBN 8046-0797-4

Manufactured by Taylor Publishing Company   Dallas, Texas

KENNIKAT SERIES IN IRISH HISTORY AND CULTURE

PREFACE

———◇———

Most of the papers here reprinted were first read to audiences of young Irishmen during a period ranging from 1885 to 1893. The material arguments for Home Rule Englishmen can master for themselves. They are summed up in one principle of government, which is true in all countries and of all races—that, if you set up a ruling caste to be aliens by profession in their own country, the inevitable consequences of their ascendency will be loss of self-respect and energy, with disaffection and decay, on the part of the subjugated nation. What is called the sentimental side of Irish patriotism is not so easily understood. There are even people who have their doubts whether it is not a fiction which agitators have invented. These pages may help outsiders to understand that the passion of Irish Nationality is at least so genuine that it is of more importance than all the other elements of the Irish problem put together— that it regards arguments drawn from material success as of inferior force in the affairs of nations, and is capable of throwing material advantages to the winds altogether when they are only to be purchased at the sacrifice of national traditions and aspirations. The only merit claimed for the lectures here submitted to English eyes is, that they admit strangers to the inner sanctuary of the Irish cause, and afford them some glimpse of the ideals which captivate youth and age alike in Ireland, and to which so much generous passion and self-sacrifice are consecrated, generation after generation.

One other remark has to be made. It is one of the stock taunts of the Unionists that Irish representatives address meetings in Ireland in language which they dare not bring under the eyes of Englishmen. The first of these lectures was delivered before a complete understanding with any English party on the question of Home Rule seemed possible. They were all prepared for audiences of young Nationalists, the most hot-blooded, perhaps, to be found in the island, and assuredly the least capable of listening without protest to doctrines which they did not fully share. They are republished here without any, even verbal, alteration. However modest may be their pretensions as to form, these lectures may, therefore, claim to represent the feelings of the youth of Ireland in their full intensity and sincerity. Englishmen may find it instructive to note how completely the passionate national aspirations of the days before Mr. Gladstone's policy was promulgated have come to harmonise with sentiments of kinship with the British people, without losing anything of their own native tenderness and enchantment for young Irishmen.

WILLIAM O'BRIEN.

November 2, 1893.

CONTENTS

———◆◇◆———

THE IRISH NATIONAL IDEA [1]

SOME time ago a leading English statesman made the extraordinary statement that he could not see why four millions of people in Ireland should have any better right to a Parliament of their own than four millions of people within the metropolitan area of London. That appeared to me a revolting way of looking at a question which has been consecrated by the hopes and the sufferings and the best blood of twenty generations of men. In fact, Mr. Chamberlain need not go a bit further than his own declaration to prove what a very considerable difference there may be between our four millions and his four millions, and how hard it is for the most painstaking of English Radicals to understand us; because, I have no doubt he would be greatly surprised to hear that, in the eyes of the Irish people, his way of dealing with the aspirations of our venerable and ancient race is more repulsive than Cromwell's. Cromwell, at all events, understood that we were flesh and blood—men with a country and a creed, with something in the hearts and souls within them—that made them proud to die for Ireland under his sword and cannon. Mr. Chamberlain treats nations as if they were casual wards in one huge workhouse. There he has us all ticketed and numbered, and clad in the same dingy uni-

[1] Presidential Address delivered before the Cork Young Ireland Society, 1885.

* B

forms, and he can't understand for the life of him what more we can desire in life than to be fed at regular hours by England, who is, of course, to be always matron of the establishment.

An English country yokel, who was once asked what was his idea of eternal happiness, is said to have replied 'Swinging on a gate munching bread and cheese.' Well, there is no accounting for tastes. It may be our misfortune that we cannot rise to the ambition of keeping the English gentleman on the gate company for all eternity, but what are we to think of the statesmanship that can see no difference between Hodge's way of looking at life and Lord Edward Fitzgerald's or Thomas Davis's? How are you to argue with a man who thinks that Irishmen can stand upon the battlefield of Benburb and ask their hearts no other question than how the land is rented about there, or, on the slopes of Vinegar Hill, experience as little emotion as if they were cockney vestrymen agitating for a new street or a main sewer through Ludgate Hill? There are five hundred bells in London which chime just as melodiously, and tell the hour with, perhaps, rather more accuracy than the Bells of Shandon. According to Mr. Chamberlain a bell is a bell, whether it tolls through the fogs of the Thames or floats over the pleasant waters of the river Lee. It is simply so many hundredweight of bell-metal hammered together for the purpose of telling all nations impartially what o'clock it is, and the only reason why a utilitarian philosopher should think more of one than of another is that it is a better timekeeper. But what Corkman has ever wandered about that seething, heartless, mighty London city, and heard the crash and jangle of bells through the murky air all around him, without feeling that in all that brazen opera of steeples there was no message that could steal into the sanctuary of his heart like one note from the bells

> Whose sounds so wild would
> In the days of childhood
> Fling round his cradle their magic spell.

It is just the same with all the other emotions of the Irish heart. You can no more impart the subtle enchantment of home to a parliament or a government in London than you could transfer the potency of the Shandon bells to a London belfry, even if you were to transfer the bells. I do not envy the mental structure of the man who could read a page of Irish history, or even cast his eye over an Irish landscape, without understanding that the Irish cause is not a mere affair of vulgar parish interests, but is woven as inextricably around the Irish heart as the network of arteries through which it draws its blood, and the delicate machinery of nerves by which it receives and communicates its impulses. That cause has all the passionate romance and glow of love. It is invested with something of the mysterious sanctity of religion. No knight of chivalry ever panted for the applause of beauty with a prouder love-light in his eyes than the flashing glance with which men have welcomed their death-wound to the fierce music of battle for Ireland. The dungeons in which innumerable Irishmen have grown gaunt and grey with torment are illuminated by a faith only less absorbing than the ethereal light of the cloister, and by visions only less entrancing.

The passion of Irish patriotism is blent with whatever is ennobling and divine in our being, with all that is tenderest in our associations, and most inspiring in the longings of our hearts. It dawns upon us as sweetly as the memory of the first gaze of a mother's loving eyes. It

is the whispered poetry of our cradles. It is the song
that is sung by every brook that gurgles by us, for every
brook has been in its day crimsoned with the blood of
heroes. It is the weird voice we hear from every
graveyard where our fathers are sleeping, for every Irish
graveyard contains the bones of uncanonised saints and
martyrs. When the framers of the penal laws denied us
books, and drew their thick black veil over Irish history,
they forgot that the ruins they had themselves made were
the most eloquent schoolmasters, the most stupendous
memorials of a history and a race that were destined not
to die. They might give our flesh to the sword, and our
fields to the spoiler, but before they could blot out the
traces of their crimes, or deface the title-deeds of our
heritage, they would have had to uproot to their last scrap
of sculptured filagree the majestic shrines in which the old
race worshipped; they would have had to demolish to their
last stone the castles which lay like wounded giants
through the land to mark where the fight had raged the
fiercest ; they would have had to level the pillar towers,
and to seal up the sources of the holy wells. And even then
they would not have stilled the voice of Ireland's past ; for
in a country where every green hill-side has been a battlefield, and almost 'every sod beneath our feet a soldier's
sepulchre,' the very ghosts would rise up as witnesses
through the penal darkness, and to the Irish imagination
the voices of the night winds would come, laden with the
memories of wrongs unavenged, and of a strife unfinished,
and of a hope which only brightened in suffering, and
which no human weapon could subdue.

The Celtic race is a race ruled by its spiritual instincts
rather than by those more ravenous virtues which we
share with the hogs and the wolves, and a race clad in the

beamy celestial armour of faith and hope is imperishable, no matter how disarmed, bare, and degraded in the eyes of a triumphant soldiery or of a more ruthless legislature. In the darkest hour of the Penal night, when it was transportation to learn the alphabet, and when Irishmen were rung outside the gates of Irish cities like lepers at sundown by the sound of the evening bell, it is not too much to say that the one simple little treason-song, 'The Blackbird,' sung low around the winter fireside in the mountain shieling, had more influence in preserving the spirit of Irish nationality than all the enactments of the diabolical penal code, enforced by all the might of England, could counteract. What the star that shone over Bethlehem on the first Christmas night was to the three Eastern Magi; what the vision of the Holy Grail was to the Knights of the Round Table; what the Holy Sepulchre was to the dying eyes of the Crusaders fainting in the parched Syrian desert, that to the children of the Irish race was and is the tradition that there has been, and the faith that there will be, a golden-hearted Irish nation—the land of song and wit and mirth and learning and holiness, and all the fair flowering of the human mind and soul. By the light of that message, glinting out in ineffaceable rainbow colours, no matter what angriest storm-clouds may cross the Irish sky, generation after generation have marched gaily to their doom upon battle-field or scaffold; and the statesman who hopes to settle accounts with Ireland by mending our clothes, and giving us an additional meal a day, without satisfying that imperious spiritual craving of the high-strung Celtic nature, may as well legislate for a time when the green hills of holy Ireland will wear the red livery of England, and when the birds on the Irish bushes will chirp 'Rule Britannia.'

Conquering nations of the coarse material texture of the
ancient Romans and the modern English have never been
able to understand why little nations like Ireland should
cling to their own hopes and ideals, instead of embracing
the new gods and scrambling for their share of the world-
wide empire which they have had the same share in building
up that the hundreds of thousands of slaves who perished
under King Rameses' lash had in building the Great Pyramid.   I have no doubt that King Xerxes' courtiers were
just as much disgusted at Leonidas' folly in standing to
be killed in the Pass of Thermopylæ, with his absurd little
mob of three hundred men, instead of sensibly coming over
to dinner with the glittering hosts of the Persians and
sharing the good things that were going, as the ordinary
Englishman is with our obstinacy in dreaming of a National
Parliament, instead of learning sense and taking our pull
out of the Hindoos and carrying all before us in the Civil
Service.   But, as a matter of historical fact, it is to small
States that the world owes its laws, its fine arts, its learning, its religion, its music, its paintings, and all the finer
elements of its civilisation, while the great military
empires of the Macedonians, and the Persians, and the
Scythians, and the Tartars have passed over the earth
and left no traces but hecatombs of bones.   Furthermore,
I cannot recall a single instance in which the genius of
a small State has been successfully transfused into the
more splendid empires which absorbed them.   The little
State which gave the world Aristotle, and Socrates, and
Demosthenes, and Praxiteles, while its genius was nursed
in freedom within a territory less than that of the county
of Cork, produced nothing better than the *Græculi esurientes*
—the little Greek pimps of Roman satire—when its
enslaved children were bribed to Rome to minister to the

glory and luxury of their conquerors. The Italian city republics, which, while their citizens numbered less than the burgess roll of Cork city, conquered the East and discovered the West, and made Italy blossom like a rose garden up to the mountain crests—the tiny States which glittered with immortal names, such as those of Dante and Da Vinci and Michael Angelo and Columbus, as under a shower of stars so long as they were free—were struck with barrenness and desolation the moment they became incorporated in the great realm of Austria. In our own century little Belgium, which as an annexe of the French Empire withered and decayed, has in one generation of autonomy sprung into an activity which confronts English trade in Birmingham and Sheffield, and has outstripped Europe in the race for the wealth of the dim regions of equatorial Africa.

Had Ireland, too, no capabilities for increasing the sum of human happiness which were shrivelled up under the blight of English domination? Has she no seeds of greatness in her bosom to-day which want but to be touched by the rays of her own unimprisoned genius to burst forth into the glory of flower and fruit? We have two tests such as no other race that I know of can answer so well—her deeds in her day of freedom, and her vitality after seven centuries of wasting bondage. The Irish race have never had fair-play. Their growth as a nation was mutilated at the moment when all the other States of modern Europe were struggling out of chaos. Judging Ireland by her state at the Norman Conquest is like judging English Parliamentary institutions by the condition of the Saxon churls after the battle of Hastings, or the civilisation of Rome by the days when an emperor was stabbed or poisoned every other year by his palace guards. Yet, if we confine our judgment of Ireland to those centuries from the coming of St. Patrick to the Danish invasions—centuries during which the other nations of Europe were simply shifting camps of savages—we shall find Ireland the sanctuary and the only uncontaminated fountain of civilisation, and a civilisation all the more marvellous that it was not derived from Rome or Greece, but grew up of its own native vigour, like a violet in some unvisited dell. Human history furnishes no fairer picture than that of Ireland in her golden age—the one lustrous star in an European night. Her people enjoyed the equality of a modern republic. Their chiefs were of their own choice. The lands belonged to the whole people. A system of law prevailed so mild that the bard was the most formidable power in the community. The sound of festivities in their halls, the chant of a thousand saints in their thousand churches, the enthusiasm of learning that lighted their schools, come down to us across the gloomy gulf of ages that followed, and make us doubt whether modern civilisation, with all its new-fangled refinements, but redoubled cares, can give us anything to compare with the simple happiness of that old race, with their bright wits, their mirthful hearts, the sensitive organisation which could be ruled by the power of music, and the glorious enthusiasm which inspired them to bear the torch of religion and learning to the ends of a darkened world. Ireland's laws, religion, arts, and hospitality were combined with a colonising capacity beyond any seen since the days of the Greek migrations to Ionia and Sicily, and with a warlike vigour which for 300 years enabled her to withstand the attacks of the terrible Northmen who overran England with as much facility as the Anglo-Saxons and

the Romans had done before them. The Scottish highlands are peopled to this day with an Irish colony as
strongly marked with the characteristics of their origin as
if the lamp of St. Columbkille still shone from the cliffs
of Iona, and the footsteps of the saints and scholars who
formed the Irish army of civilisation may still be tracked
in lines of light into the heart of the Swiss Alps and to
the furthest shores of Sicily. The marvel is not that Irish
Civilisation after struggling manfully through three centuries of Danish barbarism should have been unable to
face seven centuries more of English savagery, but that a
book, or a man, or even a ruin, of the race should survive
to tell the tale after ten centuries of unceasing battle for
the bare life.

But not only has the Irish race survived that black
deluge of suffering and plunder which for seven hundred years submerged the land. It emerges from that
long eclipse with youth renewed, with strength redoubled,
with hope undimmed, and with all the mental and moral
capacities of a great nation, only braced and rejuvenated
by sufferings that would have broken the spirit and
debased the soul of any other nation. This second youth
and vigour more robust than the first, after so horrifying
an abyss of years, is a phenomenon of which history gives
us no other example. The restored Greece of to-day is
to the Greece of Pericles what the prowling Arabs who
pilfer the Egyptian Pyramids are to the magnificent
monarchs who built them. The creatures who dwell
around the ruins of the Coliseum still call themselves
Romans, and masquerade in the grave-clothes of their
august ancestors; but nobody expects new Ciceros to
arise among the degenerate chatterers of the Corso, or
new Cæsars to shake the world from the puny throne of

the Quirinal. The Irish race of to-day, on the contrary, take up their mission just where English aggression cut it short seven centuries ago, and leap to their feet as buoyantly as though the whole hideous tragedy of the intervening ages were but the nightmare of an uneasy sleeper. The same sanguine blood bounds in their veins; the same hopes here and hereafter inspire them; the rosy freshness that suffused the morning sky of the race still kisses the hill-tops of the future as tranquilly as though its radiance had never been buried in the lightnings and the blood-red rain of ghastly centuries. There is here no taint of intellectual or physical degeneracy. The same faith that once inhabited the ruined shrines is rebuilding them. The same passion for valour, beauty, spirituality, learning, hospitality, and all that is adventurous abroad and affectionate at home, is still the badge and cognisance of the Celtic race. They are the same passionate, stormy-souled, kindly-hearted, fighting, worshipping, colonising and lightning-witted race of Ireland's golden prime, with this substantial difference, that instead of being a million of people in scattered pastoral clans, buried in this island, they are now twenty millions, doing the work and the soldiering and the statesmanship and the sacred shepherd-ing of three continents; and, whether in Australian mines or in Canadian woods, bound to this small island by stronger links than if Ireland were a despot that could stretch out a world-wide sceptre to enforce their allegiance. The Celtic race to-day is, in fact, as conspicuous a factor in human society as the Teutonic. It is little less in numbers; it is as distinct in type; it has as rich a range of capacities, sympathies, and ideals of its own; its fine susceptibilities and aerial genius are capable of exerting a potent and saving influence upon an age which seems only too ready to accept this world as a gross feeding-trough at which happiness consists in greedy gorging. There are signs that English statesmen are beginning to realise that a race such as that may be conciliated, but may by no possibility be blotted out. There are signs that the genius of the Celtic race is about to be restored to its natural throne, and to receive its natural development. God grant it! Mere surly vengeance, for vengeance sake, has never been a passion of the Irish heart. There are many nations whose arms and arts and prosperity stand indebted to the Irish race. There is not one that owes us a grudge for a deed of wanton offence or aggression. Our quarrel even with England is bounded by her rule within the shores of Ireland. The man who would rashly thwart any effort of statesmanship to tranquillise the dark and blood-stained passions that have raged for many an evil century between conquering England and unconquerable Ireland would assume a responsibility which I, for one, and I believe this audience, would shrink from sharing. But, looking back now, as calmly as an Irishman may, over the appalling gulf of years, since the first attempt of England to subjugate this island—counting its confiscations all over again, realising the horrors of all its massacres, pierced with the agony and humiliation of all that endless, hopeless strife—it is my firm persuasion that the Irish race of to-day would drain that bitter cup again, would tread that national Calvary of shame and torment all over again, would plunge back once more into that night of horrors which seemed to know no dawning, would welcome the axe and the gibbet and the battlefield once more, rather than surrender in this their hour of strength and pride the mission which their fathers have bequeathed to them with the blood in their veins—the mission of vindicating their despised and trampled race, and of giving Celtic genius once more a home and a throne in the bosom of a disenthralled and regenerated Irish nation.

THE LOST OPPORTUNITIES OF THE
IRISH GENTRY

MAY it please your Grace, my Lord Mayor, Ladies, and Gentlemen,—I cannot tell you how deeply I feel this wonderful scene of enthusiasm around me here to-night. I should be more or less than human if my heart was not thrilled to the core by the kindness which my fellow-countrymen have extended to me—kindness which I think Irishmen have never failed yet to extend to any man that they believed was doing his honest best for Ireland. I suppose it is at a moment like this that a man is particularly sensitive about such matters; but I do, indeed, desire in the most earnest words that I can command to express my gratitude to this enormous audience, and in a very special manner to express my gratitude to your Grace for the courage you have shown in taking your place amongst us here to-night, and for the noble and touching, and, I am afraid, all too generous, words that you have spoken about my humble self. I have a very miserable and haunting consciousness that I will stand in need of all your indulgence and of all your good-nature to-night, because I must tell you candidly that I have had something to do of late besides preparing ornamental lectures.

¹ Lecture delivered in the Leinster Hall, Dublin, on September 8, 1887, on the night before the Mitchelstown massacre and the prosecution of the lecturer. The Archbishop of Dublin presided.

At all events, I do hope that upon this occasion charity [1] and Mr. Balfour combined—well, the combination is certainly a strange one, but I do hope that on this occasion they will combine to form a spell sufficiently powerful to disarm your criticism and to enable me to get at the soft side of your Irish hearts to-night. I may as well mention at once that those who may expect me to develop any controversy about a round table conference,[2] or, indeed, any other so burning a topic, will be wofully disappointed. I do not mean to touch upon any topic of that sort. I think I may say that your Grace has not stated with more emphasis than the truth would warrant, that I should be the last person in Ireland to place any wanton obstacle or myself in any way to stand in the way of a suggestion which I know, and which all the world knows, except the editor of the London *Times,* has come from a brave and unflinching Irish heart as well as a capacious and states-manlike intellect. Your Grace has quite correctly antici-pated that I intend to speak only of the opportunities that the Irish gentry have lost—and madly lost—in the past, and that I do not speak—I shall not say even that I despair— of the opportunities that may yet be within their grasp.

The hour is never too late for Irish forgiveness—even for the class whose hands I am sorry to say are to this hour red with evictions, and whose voices are still hoarse with clamour for coercion. What I intend to do—and what, I trust, when you have heard me, your Grace will agree with me that it is a healthy thing and a wholesome thing in the interest both of the Irish people and the Irish gentry to do, is to point out that it is the Irish gentry themselves

[1] The lecture was for the benefit of a Dublin charity.

[2] A proposal made by the Archbishop of Dublin at the time for a friendly conference with the Irish landlords.

who have taught us to do without them—who have forced us to do without them and to defy them ; and what I mean to point out is that they must not be surprised if now and for evermore we base our confidence for the future of our country upon the might and the organisation of the democracy of Ireland, and upon the sympathy and the co-operation of the democracy of England. That is the scope of the remarks that I shall offer to this assembly here to-night.

I remember, not so very long ago, ' democracy ' used to be thought an awful, almost a naughty, word among genteel people in Ireland. Some of us had no more conception what sort of uncouth animal a democrat was than Mrs. Partington had of the attributes of the allegory on the Nile. Irishmen were supposed to be nothing if not admirers of the old aristocracy. If you were to believe Charles Lever's novels, a man who was of ancient lineage might, without detriment to his popularity, desolate a whole countryside, he might beggar his tenants, and mortgage his property up to the eyes, he might get drunk every night of his life, and put a bullet through an unfortunate tradesman if he asked for payment of his bill. The Irish people were supposed rather to like that sort of thing from a gentleman of spirit, and the people put their hands to their hats for him, and voted for him, and fought for him, as if it were the best fun in the world to be evicted and swindled by one of ' the old stock.' It is the irony of fate that the very practices which the Irish gentry rebuke with a celestial grace in the Irish peasants of to-day as crimes of the blackest dye are only faint imitations of the pastimes of their own fathers and grandfathers. Tarring a bailiff and making him swallow his own latitats is a proceeding copied from the highest aristocratic precedents. Mr. George Robert Fitzgerald was by no means the only man who mounted cannon upon his castle to give the ministers of the law a hotter reception than they encountered at Bodyke and Coolgreany. It was the regular way of discharging honest debts in well-bred circles. The noble family of Kingston, who are at this moment so horrified by the people of Mitchelstown barricading their homes and defending them, were themselves for many a day 'Sunday men,' and kept their castles provisioned for a siege. It is, indeed, because they did so, and left their debts unpaid—the debts they incurred to pamper their own bodies and fuddle their brains—that their noble descendant is now engaged in exterminating the unfortunate tenantry of Mitchelstown, not for repudiating any honest debt, but because they will not surrender the homes in which their fathers lived and died, and the lands that are watered with their sweat, to pay for the claret and the dissipations of those old 'wolves of the Galtees.'

But, undoubtedly, the people did not like the Irish gentry the less for their contempt for the law and their way of dealing with bailiffs. Aristocracy was respected to almost adoration point. I remember, when we were young fellows long ago in my native town of Mallow, we used to think the Clubhouse there a kind of seventh heaven, inhabited by beings of quite another order from mere people who worked for a living. It seemed as much a dispensation of Providence as that the sun should rise in the heavens every day that the gentry should lord it over us and look down on us. It seemed part of the order and arrangement of the universe. Well, I think we have somewhat moderated these gentlemen's estimate of their own importance. I can hardly ever pass that Clubhouse now without thinking that there is not a cabin in the poor suburb of Ballydaheen whose inmates have not as much influence upon the current of affairs as the whole galaxy of gentlemen who assemble on the Clubhouse steps put together. Now, what is the reason of this extraordinary transformation? I often think that one of the bitterest reflections of the Irish gentry in these days of humiliation and helplessness must be that it is all their own fault—that they had the country and people for hundreds of years like potter's clay in their hands. If they had chosen to be the people's chiefs and leaders instead of being their slave-drivers, the Irish aristocracy might have had a great career. Unquestionably, rank and brilliancy and chivalry, and all the qualities that appertain to a privileged, leisured class, have always had a fascination for the Irish people. Men of that class who, instead of standing apart in cold and haughty isolation, have given their hearts and lives to the rescue of their down-trodden nation, are the heroes and idols of our history—men like Sarsfield, Grattan, Lord Edward Fitzgerald, Davis, Smith O'Brien, and Charles Stewart Parnell. Did the Irish people ever ask what was these men's religious faith, or in what century their ancestors came over? The Geraldines when they settled long ago in Mallow Castle did not shut themselves up in a clubhouse, and give themselves airs. They fraternised with the people, they made themselves bone of their bone and flesh of their flesh ; they fought for them and died with them.. And I wonder which is the nobler field of ambition— which is the more likely to shed lustre upon or give stability to an aristocracy—the career of one of those Geraldines ruling like a king over every peasant from Listowel to the Galtee Mountains, or the career of the present head of the Geraldines, barricaded in his castle at Carton, composing pamphlets for the I.L.P.U., and unable to return a poor-law guardian for his own electoral division?

C

I venture to think that, though the present Geraldine is a duke, and the old Geraldines used sometimes to have a head chopped off, most of us would prefer to take chance with the valiant old chiefs who died with their faces to the foe and with their clans around them, fighting for their God and for their native land. If ever men were petted as leaders, and besought to become leaders of the Irish people, it was the Irish gentry. It was one of the foibles, perhaps one of the vices, of the Irish people, their fondness and yearning for leaders of birth and station. The aristocrats who led the Volunteers of '82, with the exception of Grattan and half a dozen others, were bigots and rack-renters, who had very little to recommend them except their volunteer uniform ; yet their popularity knew no bounds. O'Connell tried to keep the Catholic lords and aristocrats in the van of the Emancipation movement, until his heart was sick of their cowardice, and meanness, and sycophancy—they have never to this day been emancipated in their souls. The Young Ireland movement was very largely a movement with aristocratic aspirations. Mitchel and Lalor, indeed, knew the stuff the Irish gentry were made of, but most of the generous-hearted young men who sang and spoke in those days did not despair of bringing the gentry into the National ranks, and building up a nation in which landlord and tenant would clasp hands and blend as harmoniously as orange and green. One of the most amazing things we learn from Sir Charles Gavan Duffy's book, ' Four Years of Irish History,' is that up to the very eve of the revolt of '48 Smith O'Brien and some of his colleagues nourished the extraordinary delusion that the Irish gentry were meditating going over *en masse* to the young men who were counting their pikes and guns for an insurrection. It was O'Brien's noble fault to believe everyone to be as open-hearted and as chivalrous as himself. He actually wrote letters anticipating that the gentry would be found heading the insurrection at the very moment when these same gentry were entreating Dublin Castle to suspend the Habeas Corpus Act ; and only a few weeks before his own brother, Sir Lucius O'Brien, denounced and disowned him as a traitor on the floor of the House of Commons. Every opportunity the Irish aristocracy ever got of identifying themselves with the people, of winning their affections, of becoming their leaders, they spurned with insult and disdain. They repaid their popularity in the Volunteer times by their murderings and burnings and floggings in '98. Their answers to all the melting appeals of the orators and singers of Young Ireland was to seize the crops for the rent while two millions of people were dying of famine, and then to exterminate a million more of them between 1848 and 1853, when all national spirit was extinguished, and when the country lay gasping and helpless at their feet. Even in our own day, in the midst of the angry rush and roar of the revolution which their own folly brought about their ears, the Irish gentry obtained at least three separate opportunities of harmonising their interests with those of the country of their birth and the people from whom they derived their living. It is one of the most astounding facts in the history of human fatuity that the immediate and proximate cause of the Land League movement in the County Mayo was a confederacy of four of the greatest landowners in the county—Lord Lucan, Sir Roger Palmer, Sir Robert Blosse Lynch, and Lord Sligo— to refuse a wretched abatement of only 10 per cent. to a tenantry on the brink of starvation. They kept their 10 per cent., and they founded the Land League. I re-

member with what shrieks of laughter the landlord newspapers received the first project of the Land League, under
Mr. Parnell's hand, to buy the landowners out at twenty
years' purchase of Griffith's valuation. I wonder what
they would give to catch Mr. Parnell's signature to such
an offer under date of this present month of grace,
September, 1887. I am afraid it is only an artist from
the *Times* Office who is likely to furnish them with such
a document. Again, several years ago, in a remarkable
paper read before the Statistical Society, Lord Monteagle
suggested to the landlords of Ireland the two conditions,
and the only two conditions, on which they could still lead
lives of comfort and of honour and of usefulness in their
native land—First, that they should cease to be landlords;
second, that they should cease to act as the English garrison. That is, of course, the landlord way of putting it.
What acting as the English garrison really means is using
the power of England to garrison their own rent offices
and to make the name of England detestable; for I deny
that the landlords of Ireland have ever been either a loyal
or an efficient garrison of England, whenever their own
interests or their own fears prompted them to be rebels or
runaways. Well, Lord Monteagle's warning fell on heed-
less ears. Mr. Gladstone's great Bills of last year came.
They offered the most splendid avenue to power and honour
that ever opened its arms to a dethroned and fallen oligarchy. The Irish gentry might have had a price for their
estates which, in a cheap country like Ireland, would have
ensured them affluence. They might have had in the Parliament of their country the power for which they hunger
and which they travel all the way from the Riviera to retain
in even a local board of guardians. Far-seeing men have
estimated that in an Irish Parliament, constituted according

to Mr. Gladstone's scheme, a wise and capable and patriotic
Conservative party might not only have been a potential
minority, but might have found their way to an Irish
Treasury Bench. And all this upon the one simple condition of fusing their interests and sympathies with those
of the body of their countrymen, instead of for ever fever-
ing and distempering their country like an angry pustule
or like a poisoned spear-point. Did the Irish people look
surly or haggle about the price ? On the contrary, they
pined and yearned for peace and brotherhood, in the great
task of building up a happy Irish nation. And the Irish
gentry ? With a few noble exceptions, such as Lord
Powerscourt and Lord Greville, their answer was to smite
the hand that was extended to them. Their answer was
to summon the demons of religious bigotry from their den,
and to circulate eleven millions of scurrilous libels on their
fellow-countrymen through the printing-press of the Irish
Loyal and Patriotic Union.

They complain a great deal nowadays of our setting
class against class. It was they themselves, in their blind
arrogance and folly, in spite of the prayers and the warn-
ings and the entreaties of Irish Nationalists—it was they
themselves who first set class against class, or rather set
up their own selfish and pampered class against the
interests and sympathies and the aspirations of every other
class in the nation. They never, as a class, established one
idea in common with the people upon whose industry they
lived. They remain to this day as distinctly foreigners in
race and language and sympathy as when their ancestors
came over, throat-cutting and psalm-singing, with Cromwell. They had three hundred years of unbroken power
to make history, and the history they made was a history
of famines and rack-rents and penal laws and misery—a

history of millions plundered and degraded in their own
land under the heel of a few thousand foreigners—a history
of ages during which the gentry of Ireland never did an
act of justice that was not wrung from them, and never
did one act of unadulterated grace so long as England
gave them her bayonets to enable them to refuse it.

Nemesis came at last in the shape of an Irish democracy,
and it is a singular fact that democracy is a Frankenstein
of their own raising.   Democracy has sprung from the
two very sources which England relied upon to rid her of
the Irish difficulty—National education and emigration.
The National system of Education was founded for the
express purpose of undermining the faith and destroying
the nationality of the youth of Ireland.   Men like Archbishop Whately and Mr. Carlile, who devised that system,
and who composed the school-books, were dead certain
that they had discovered a machine for turning the youth
of Ireland into soupers in faith and West Britons in
politics.   Things have not turned out quite to their satisfaction.   Sir R. Peel relied on two instruments to de-
nationalise Ireland—the policeman and the schoolmaster.
Whatever the constabulary system did to enchain the
limbs of the Irish people, his system of National Education
did still more to emancipate their minds and souls.   The
policeman proved to be an efficient ally of England, but
the schoolmaster did not turn out so satisfactorily, and
the schoolmaster is the more potent man of the two when
all is said and done.   It is the young fellows whom
the governing classes sent into the national schools to be
turned into flunkeys and slaves—it is these very young
fellows who have broken the power of the privileged classes
in Ireland, and pushed them from their thrones, and
bearded them at the poor-law boards and the municipal

boards, and even on the floor of the House of Commons. In the same way the Irish gentry believed that the policy of emigration was a stroke of genius to deliver them from a troublesome population. They believed that once the Irish peasant was embarked in a coffin-ship, they were done with him for evermore. But there came back from America a power more fatal to aristocracy and to privileged idleness than if these Irish emigrants had come back in line-of-battle ships and armies. There came back the principles of democracy and freedom which the emigrants imbibed in the great Republic of the West. Every American letter that came home was a lesson in democracy.

From the time that American principles took root here in the soil that was prepared for them by education, it was all over with the ascendency of the Irish gentry ; for, from the moment free inquiry began to be focussed upon them, their pretensions melted away like wax before a fire. People began to ask themselves who were these gods who wrapped themselves up in cold and haughty majesty, and looked down upon the people whose industry gave them rents to squander and purple and fine linen to bask in. To our surprise we found that they were not gods, but men, with blood very much the same colour as other men's, and with a by no means alarming preponderance of brains. The gods were, in fact, a squad of Cromwellian troopers a few generations removed. As somebody remarked—I think it was O'Connell—the Irish gentry have nothing ancient about them but their prejudices, and nothing modern except their pedigrees. The so-called ' old families ' were but things of yesterday compared with the ancient race they despised and lorded it over. The real old families of the land are to be found not in the landlords' mansion, but in the cabins of their serfs.   To have remained rich and flourishing during a history such as ours is the greatest reproach a native family could incur. In a history like that of the Irish race poverty is the best sign of nobility, and rank is the best evidence of shame.

When thoughts of this kind began to work and burn in the minds of the young men of Ireland, their revolt against the supremacy of this alien caste was as sudden as their submissiveness had been complete. I remember even within our own time the first of the elected poor law-law guardians who were taken from the ranks of the people—how they used to slouch into the board-room in a shame-faced, apologetic kind of way, how they used to slide into a seat as far away from ' the gentlemen ' as possible, and sit on the edge of the chair, and vote like sheep, and hardly ever venture a remark. I saw the new spirit of manhood and of self-respect that came into these men when they rose and measured themselves like men with these noble lords and gentlemen, and routed them from their dignities, and told them to their faces that the day of aristocratic privilege was gone, and the power of the people, and the welfare of the people, must henceforth be more important elements in the government of mankind than coronets or Norman blood.

If you go into the Irish board-room of an Irish board of guardians now, you won't find the elected guardians trembling under the frown of the ex-officios ; it is rather the other way. If you listen to a debate in the House of Commons, you won't find men of the people like Mr. Healy or Mr. Sexton grovelling at the feet of the King-Harmans and Saundersons, or speaking with bated breath because every second man who is listening to him has a title or a million of money.

I never will forget the expression of a little old Western peasant at one of the Land League meetings, when some speaker was describing the oppression and the haughtiness of the Irish land-agents in the past—' Begob,' said the old fellow, ' we'll make them put their hands to their hats for us yet.' That really only describes in a comically exaggerated way the change that has come over the face of the country ; for, though the Irish people are of too generous and forgiving and Christian a character ever to desire to retort upon their opponents the indignities that were inflicted upon themselves, still it was necessary to enforce the lesson—and I think the lesson is beginning to impress itself upon the comprehension of the most fossilised old gentleman in the land—that a man's importance and his place in the esteem of his fellow-countrymen will depend for the future in Ireland, not upon the length of his purse, nor the length of his pedigree, but upon his usefulness to the community and his readiness to labour and to sacrifice himself for the benefit of his fellow-countrymen. Up to the present, by an extraordinary perversion of the law of nature, a man's consequence in Ireland was measured by the amount of misery he created ; for the future it will be measured by the amount of happiness he can confer—the amount of good he can do in protecting industry, rewarding toil, and raising up the poor and lowly. The Irish gentry have, fortunately for human rights, left us no alternative but to be democrats and to draw our strength from the great heart of the people.

There is one thing upon which I think we may fairly congratulate ourselves in reference to the spread of democracy, and that is, that democracy, as it is rooted in Ireland to-day, is almost altogether free from the features of bloodthirstiness and rabid class hatred and irreligion

which have sometimes made revolution a name of dread
and horror in other lands. The Irish people have not the
slightest dislike to a man merely because he has a good
coat to his back, or because he comes of an ancient family.
The objection to Mr. Parnell's class is that it produces
only one Mr. Parnell to ten thousand aliens or enemies
and oppressors of the people. If in the morning the Irish
gentry proposed frankly to draw a wet sponge over the
past, there is not a prominent politician in Ireland who
would answer with a churlish or contumelious word. They
would be welcomed. They would be honoured. The Irish
nature has the softness of our own honeyed meads—

There is dew at high noontide there, and springs in the yellow sands,
On the fair hills of holy Ireland.

Irish forgiveness is to be had to this hour for the honest
asking. A single Smith O'Brien redeems a whole pedigree
of Murrough the Burners and Black Inchiquins.

The change which the wizardry of one great old man
has wrought in the course of a single year in the feelings
of the most extreme of us towards the English people is
an assurance that no prejudices are too ancient, no wrongs
too cruel, no grudges too deep-seated, to yield to the first
appeal which English genius and sincerity have ever
made to the infinite tenderness of the Irish heart.
There will be false gods no more in Ireland ; but for
good men and capable men who have a heart for the
miseries of their countrymen and the will to labour for
their alleviation, there is still, and there will be always,
welcome, honour, and gratitude, no matter what their
class or from what race they may have sprung. But the
longer the Irish gentry continue at enmity with the Irish
people the harder will be the terms of their inevitable
surrender when it comes. Forty years ago they might

become Nationalists without ceasing to be landlords. It is perfectly possible that, if the Irish landlords had been wise enough to band themselves enthusiastically with the people at that time to win an Irish Parliament, and had flooded and dominated that Parliament with their own territorial influence, their rackrents might remain un-abridged for many a day, and the enforcement of popular rights might have been indefinitely retarded. At present the Irish people can dispense with them as Nationalists, and are determined to dispense with them as landlords. I have claimed that Irish democracy is not bloodthirsty or vengeful. If those who are so fond of magnifying the deeds of violence which have blotted our history here and there for the last few years would only examine the dark story of revolution in other lands, and think of the seas of suffering and bloodshed which engulf the beaten side—if they will only remember how their own class used their victory when they tortured and trampled to death tens of thousands of the Wexford insurgents in '98—they will have to confess that there never was a revolution involving the overthrow of so rooted and so detested an oligarchy which was effected at so small a cost of bloodshed and crime as ours, and they will have to confess that, whatever crime lurked in the train of that great and memorable peaceful revolution was not the outgrowth of democracy, but was a remnant of the barbarism their own oppression had begotten. Finally, the revolutionary spirit of Ireland is not sullied by irreligion upon one side, or by sectarian bigotry on the other. It has a heart equally large and equally warm for Protestant and for Catholic—for every man who has a heart or hand for Ireland. It is, at the same time, in the highest and deepest sense religious, spiritual, and above the ignoble empire of materialism,

and contains no taint or germ of that crazy Continental
fanaticism which assails the Altar as ferociously as the
Bastile, which breaks up the very foundations of society,
defiles the sanctity of the Christian household, breaks
down the glorious faith and hope that surround this
fleeting world with the wonders of eternity, and
counts the very Author of the Universe among the
enemies of man. From this bleak abyss we have been
saved by the deep and yearning spirit which teaches
the Irish people that, even when all has been done that
human devotion can do to reward industry, to alleviate
suffering and brighten human life, there still remain in
this wondrous spiritual nature of ours aspirations and
capacities which will never be satisfied in this material
world, and which will never consent to be stifled in
the grave. We have been saved, furthermore, by the
enlightened fortitude of some of those who have guided
the religious life of Ireland, one of whom is not far away
from us here to-night, and the other whose name will be
honoured by the Irish race as long as the Rock of Cashel
stands amidst the smiling plains of Tipperary. These
men have identified religion, not with the privileges and
the oppressions of the rich, but with the cause of the poor
and the hopes of the oppressed. They have shown that
no measure of equality among men, no struggle to exorcise
the demons of selfish monopoly and luxury which have
hitherto cruelly darkened the lives of the people, can be
too bold or too sweeping for the religion of Him whose
life of infinite piety was spent among the lowly, and whose
inspired Apostles were chosen from the fisherman's hut
and from the carpenter's bench, and not from the palaces
of kings and nobles. Irish democracy in our day is in
fact no new thing, but a return to the old golden days of

Ireland's greatness, when the land was the people's, and the chiefs were of the people's choice, when the sublime song of the bard, and the prayer of the monk, and the mind of the scholar, were instruments of government more powerful than the tyrant's bayonets have been ever since ; and as we push boldly on upon the path of equal rights for all and uncompromising war upon all the monopolies and privileges that still stand in the way of human happiness, the Irish democracy will, please God, never stay their march or abate their claims until the radiance of freedom which once lighted this island enwraps her again, and makes her once more the bright herald of knowledge, truth, and liberty to the world.

AMONG THE CLOUDS IN IRELAND [1]

You ask me to write about my imprisonment, but whirling as I have been for the past three days through mountain glens, whose every breeze or streamlet sings a song of liberty, there would be a certain churlishness in turning back to brood over those six months of drab monotony in Galway Gaol, behind a twenty-one-foot wall, straining for some dim murmur of the national life-and-death struggle which was raging all the while beyond. On Saturday last we were driving past the free side of that prison wall. Its grey buttresses skirt the road to Connemara. The dinner-bell—the bell that has served for a death-bell, also, pretty often in its time—was ringing our ex-companions in misfortune from the stone-yard to their mess of suet pudding or Indian-meal soup. The O'Flaherty country, in its best coat of royal heather, with patches of golden harvest plenty among its rocks, opened its hospitable arms in front of us. The prison walls receded amidst church spires and crumbling towers into mellow distance, until they looked like part of the mediæval fortification within which the Irish Jacobites made their last stand, and the notes of the prison bell melted in with the never-ending chimes and church bells which set life in Galway to the music of a dreamy Spanish chant. So let the memory of those slow-moving months,

[1] Published in the *Speaker*, August 29, 1891.

from January's ice to August's gold, fade not altogether
untenderly away into ancient history. The truth is,
Mr. Balfour's prison policy is as dead as King Cheops
under his pyramid. He (the Chief Secretary, not the
Pharaoh) began with convicts' jackets, shaved heads, and
oakum-picking for his political prisoners, with assault and
battery by half-a-dozen turnkeys for whoever objected ;
he ends by giving his ' criminals ' the run of the Galway
Queen's College Library for their reading, and supplying
them with official pens and foolscap *gratis* to write their
novels withal. The collapse of Coercion outside the prison
walls is just as notable. When I was last at liberty, my
wife and myself were pursued over the Lakes of Killarney
by policemen in boats, and over the mountains by policemen on cars and bicycles. Around the hotel where we
stayed at Glengarriff a police-car remained harnessed night
and day, a police-boat moved about the mouth of the bay,
and a police-scout on a neighbouring hill swept the hotel
grounds with a telescope. Police-bicycles, police-boats,
and police-cars have vanished with the pitch-cap and the
Penal Laws. We have actually passed for whole miles
through our own country without having so much as a
single police ' shadow ' slouching at our heels. The
ingenuity which had formerly to be employed to shake off
the nightmares in the dark grey coats and rifles has now
only to be applied to the more innocent, if more difficult,
task of evading the ' little addresses ' and the ' few words '
with which popular hospitality will insist upon enlivening
the road.

How comes the change ? It is not that the Balfour-
isation of Ireland has advanced an inch. Every tenants'
combination against which Mr. Balfour was warring when
we entered prison was as impregnable in its entrenchments

as ever when we came out. Even with the National ranks
rent asunder for nine months, and the National funds tied
up, he has not been able to snatch a single victory over
the squares of unarmed Irish tenants against whom he has
been for five years back hurling all the power of Britain
in vain. Still less, of course, has he ventured to make
himself ridiculous by starting a Tory candidate at any of
the bye-elections, even with the Nationalists ranged in
opposing camps—although only a dozen years since Carlow
and Sligo were supposed to be as safe Tory strongholds as
Mr. W. H. Smith's seat for the Strand. A generation
ago some simple-minded folk in England used to spend
hundreds of thousands of pounds on the brilliant project
of bribing ' Popery ' out of Connemara whenever the
potato blight left the hungry little Papists open to the
arguments of soup and blankets. The potatoes having failed
last year, Mr. Balfour took up the derelict work of the
Irish Church Missions, and invested hundreds of thousands
of the British taxpayer's money in a scheme of political
souperism among the distressed peasants of the West.
I heartily congratulate the poor people upon whatever
little profits will have trickled into their pockets out of
Connemara railways, road-tinkering, and the like '.relief
works.' I would even thankfully acknowledge Mr. Balfour's
liberality with the British taxpayer's alms in these poor
regions if he had not been guilty of the meanness of refusing to spend a pound in any district that did not present
him with a dutiful address, or help the local sergeant of
police to erect a triumphal arch in his honour. But, as
a measure for the conversion of Connemara from the
Nationalist heresy, his expenditures have as little to show
for themselves as the forlorn settlements of the Irish
Church Mission folk. Now that the harvest has come,

and a laughing family of potatoes answers to every stroke
of the spade, it is safe to say that Mr. Balfour's agents
could not scrape together among the peasantry of any
Parliamentary division along the distressed Western seaboard, even so many as the ten signatures that would
be necessary to fill a Tory candidate's nomination paper.
Whether he bribes in the West or coerces in the South, to
that complexion has Tory rule in Ireland come after five
years of swaggering words and evil deeds.

The Coercionists' hope is no longer in plank-beds, nor
in charitable doles through the police sergeant's hands, nor
yet in fractured skulls through the force of his bâton.   It
would be comical, if it were not to an Irishman most sad,
that their last hope lies in Mr. Parnell.   Mr. Parnell has
many as honest-hearted Irish Nationalists as breathe
among his adherents, but it is an incontrovertible fact that
every landlord, agent, removable magistrate, emergency-
man, or landgrabber in the country—every man who has
openly or covertly distinguished himself by hostility to
the Home Rule movement—has suddenly blossomed into
an ardent Parnellite.   In any first-class carriage you are
sure to meet a squire who has discovered Mr. Parnell to be
a man of genius.   The officials smack their lips over his
speeches, and devour the Parnellite journals with avidity.
To hear them talk, you would suppose that the once 'loyal
minority' were all along athirst for the pure gospel of
Irish Nationality, only that milk-and-water patriots like
John Dillon would fain force them to be content with the
muddy waters of English Whiggery.   When you see the
landlord and the Removable feasting on the *Freeman*, and
hear the Orangemen beating Mr. Parnell's praises on their
drums, all that it means, of course, is that they believe
him to be engaged in wrecking the Home Rule movement

D

with twice the zest and energy with which he built it up.
But, all the same, the complete working understanding
which this crisis has brought about between the Orange
and Green extremities of the Irish body politic disposes of
one catching argument against Home Rule. If the landowners and sons of King William can forget their grudges
against Mr. Parnell the moment they see their advantage
in linking battalions with him, who will any longer pre-
tend that in an Irish Parliament the 'loyal minority'
would not display an equally keen scent for their own
interest, and foregather with my excellent friend Mr. John
Clancy on the Opposition benches just as cheerfully as they
now dilate upon Mr. Parnell's qualities as a statesman?
As to the merits of our intestine struggle, I say nothing
here. Englishmen have shown a most wise discretion in
meddling as little as possible with our family jars. The
question of the Irish leadership is one wholly for Irish
Nationalists to settle; and they are settling in the most
wondrous manner, solemnly, tranquilly, irresistibly, by
mere votes and arguments, an organic civil strife of a kind
which in France would long ago have been argued out
with artillery, and which in England cost you two revolu-
tions when there was question of driving out a less resolute
Stuart dynasty.

In the lovely highlands whose air we have been quaffing
for the past few days the people are, politically speaking,
the same happy family as ever. Not that, even in the
deepest recesses of their cloudy mountains, there are not
keen politicians around the peat-fires. The national school
and the weekly newspaper, and, more potent than all, the
American letter, have found their way into a glen where,
even eleven years ago, I could not find man, woman, or
child who understood the English language. But the

Zeitgeist has not yet taken the bloom of simple trustfulness and veneration off the delightful mountain folk in the white flannel *baunyeens* and maddered petticoats—not, at all events, in regions outside the disenchanting track of the railways and the tourist cars.   I wish I could have devoted this communication wholly to the description of an un-travelled route between Cong and Leenane, which we happened upon last Monday, and for which the weary seeker after an unhackneyed Swiss valley would give volumes of Cook's coupons.   Men who have dipped among the misty blue mountains of the Joyce country, and been repulsed from the door of Lord Leitrim's hotel in the Alpine valley under Maamturk, where a Swiss hotel-keeper would have found a gold mine, have never discovered that away on the north side of the Maam range, Lough Mask sends up a long silver arm into the heart of the mountains around Finnæ, which, like an enchanted wand, turns all around it into romance.   The lough, now laughing like a lady's mirror, now black as an Irish famine, zigzags through glens where never tourist trod ; past patches of primeval forest that may have been waving when Queen Elizabeth's first red-coat was seen in the MacWilliam country ; past softly sculptured hills in a blaze of purple and gold, with the blossoms of the bog-asphodel and the heather ; past statelier hills, whose bases are draped in deep black, and their heads hooded with thunder clouds ; past farmhouses, whose thatch is roped down with flag-stones for fear of its being whirled across the mountains of a winter night; past marvellous little plots of tillage among the stern rocks, where the potato stalks, I am glad to say, are of a glowing, healthy green, and the oats beginning to receive their crown of modest gold—all swept by a breeze which, even with its all too frequent kiss

of clammy mist, bears health and hope and roses with
every breath to the little shoeless cherubs who lisp their
soft Gaelic at the cabin-doors, or peep like mountain goats
from their free crags at the unprecedented invaders in
their travelling-carriage.   How characteristic of English
government in Ireland that this beautiful region should
have been discovered by means of a terrible murder!
Such alas! is the case.   Some ten years ago, two bailiffs,
father and son, were murdered here in a fit of frenzy, and
their corpses cast into the lake.   In the very bosom of the
glen, the iron police-hut, which was planted there in
consequence, still stands like a black mark against the
character of the gentle-faced surroundings ; a road had to
be constructed for the accommodation of the police, and
thus the poor community, which for centuries had lain
neglected in misery and darkness, until it shed blood and
got into the newspapers, is now able to travel to market
over an excellent cart-road, and has two superb school-
houses, and is on the high-road to becoming one of the
most favoured resorts in this island.

Upon the whole there is a cheering air of improvement
beginning to blow all around.   When I was last in
Connemara (in 1879) the people were cowering in terror
of a famine which the Tory Government of the day, of
course, denounced as a Nationalist fiction, and which,
equally of course, they a few months afterwards were
spilling out a million of money in endeavouring to cope
with.   But even more awful than famine in those days
was the unbridled power of eviction and rent-raising, which
haunted every peasant's door like a black Erinnys.   It is
only now that the remote and hunger-sodden peasant of
the Wild West is beginning vaguely to realise that the
landlord has no longer the power of a Jehovah—that it is

now possible for him to improve his patch, and to have a
cosy cabin, and even to put shoes on his daughter's feet,
without the terror of a rise of rent or an eviction notice.
When I recall the people's broken and despairful looks
in 1879, and contrast them with their carriage to-day, I
doubt whether even the most thoughtful of us has yet
realised with sufficient thankfulness the fact that in the
interval there has passed over the face of Ireland a revolution, which has secured for the Irish peasantry all that,
and more than, the French Revolution secured for the
peasantry of France, and that at less cost of bloodshed in
the whole course of the struggle than the French had to
pay in any one day of their long years of bloody travail.
A woeful deal, indeed, remains to be done ; but the most
joyous feature in the Irish peasant's horoscope is the
confidence that we are only in the beginning of the better
days.

A GEM OF MISGOVERNMENT IN IRELAND [1]

CLARE ISLAND, which Imperial genius has brought lower than the wretchedness of a workhouse ward, was built by nature for one of those pleasure isles which, when they are anchored off an Italian coast, are the delight of the printers of oleographs, and off the coast of Hampshire have their value per foot run as building ground. It lies outside the tourist grooves. None but an occasional yacht's crew or a shooter of blackcock on the mountains of Achill realises the grandeur of the Mayo coast scenery which forms the island's pleasure-ground. For forty miles to the north and for thirty miles to the south the shore is piled with mountains of every imaginable romantic curve and hue, with here and there a peak towering at the very water's edge, its sea-face a mere massy ocean cliff dropping down sheer fifteen hundred feet into the foam. The ocean-front of Clare Island is just such a mountain-cliff. The eagles, and the eagles alone, can find a foothold overhead, and the base is scooped out into ocean-caves where the storms forge their thunder on winter nights, and the seals hold their uncanny parliament when the waves are in their summer sleep. The island has its proud story as well as its jewel-house of scenery. It was an independent principality up to Elizabeth's day. Its Princess, Granu Uaile, who paid

1 Published in the *Speaker*, May 7, 1892.

her royal sister a state visit at Hampton Court, patronised
the great Queen as graciously as the Emperor William
patronises his grandmother; and, in strictest historical
truth, the Irish Princess, who, throughout Spanish wars
and Irish rebellions innumerable, managed to keep her
head on her shoulders and save her dominions, and even
practise her religion to her dying day, was a woman
worthy to rank with Elizabeth and with the hapless
Queen of Scots among the heroines of those spacious
times. Grace O'Malley's profession was largely that of
pirate, which was also the profession of Franky Drake,
and, indeed, of Queen Elizabeth herself, who was only
a more cautious practitioner. All was grist that came to
her mill; a rich galleass of the Invincible Armada, which
was wrecked on the rocks of Mweelaun, an English prize-
ship which she tore from one of Drake's bull-dog captains;
or, failing such big game, a wine-ship bound for Galway,
or a Bristol merchantman's cargo of cloth. It was the
statesmanship of those days, and was only disreputable
where it failed, which was never Granu Uaile's case. The
Clare Island of the Irish Princess, at all events, had its
powerful fleet of galleys, and no stint of mountain mutton
or of Spanish wine to wash it down, three hundred years
ago.

Last year every man, woman, and child upon the
island, except the priest, the police, and the landlord's
bailiff, were in a state of starvation, and were only re-
spited by public alms from death by hunger. What a
commentary upon three hundred years of undisputed
British supremacy! Grace O'Malley's grim fortress over
the little island port has become a police barrack, where
green-coated constabularymen with repeating rifles have
set up a system of piracy more cruel and less breezy than

that of the Spanish Main. The fleet of galleys has
vanished.   The islanders, whose bards once proudly
bragged that 'there never was a good man of the
O'Malleys yet but was a mariner,' have only two five-ton
yawls to the whole island.   They have lost the art of
braving the billows, and have no means of fishing up their
dinner out of seas from which foreign trawlers are at this
moment raising tons of sole and turbot.   And the little
island that once ruled the Western seas ?   A notorious
land-jobber, who was also sub-Sheriff for the county,
bought it after the Great Famine, with a view to exterminating the remnant of the population and re-selling the
island to the Government for a convict-station.   The deal
with the Government did not come off, and the speculator
—a man with bowels of iron—recouped himself by trebling
the rents upon the tenants, in place of evicting them
root and branch.   And so the poor sons of Granu Uaile
staggered along through a generation, oscillating from
famine to dearth, and back again from dearth to famine,
until last year, in the ninety-first year of the ever-blessed
Union, Mr. Balfour's inspectors reported that the entire
population was without food or the means of buying it,
and must be either fed at the public charges or die.   The
British taxpayer was laid under contribution.   The official
return lately presented (Relief of Distress, Ireland,
1890–91) shows that relief works were set going on the
island from 23rd December to 5th August—that is to say,
until the potatoes were ripe for digging ; that at one time
93 out of a total population of 622 souls—roughly speaking, one from every household on the island—were in
receipt of weekly wages from the State ; and that in
road-making alone 813*l.* was thus expended on wages—a
comparative torrent of gold on an island whose official

valuation is only 18s. 4d. per head of the population. In addition to this, the islanders' potato-patches were planted at the expense of the Poor-Law Union. Largesse was distributed liberally out of the Balfour and Zetland Famine Fund of 40,000l. The constabulary laid aside their loaded rifles to become distributors of relief. To crown all, Lady Zetland and Miss Balfour visited the island in state, and through a corps of reporters the British public learned how the praises of Mr. Balfour were chanted by a grateful peasantry in an address which was drafted (the detail was not mentioned) by the hand of the local Removable magistrate.

A very respectable substitute, you will say, for the royal bounty of Granu Uaile. If British rule cannot choose but produce chronic famine, at least the next best thing is to encounter it with Government rations ? True, if Irish landlordism were not all the while preparing to pounce upon the Government rations as they reached the peasants' mouths, and—more amazing still—if the very Government which issued the rations did not deliberately assist in the theft.   Mark, however, what occurred.

Even while the relief works were in full swing, the landlord's agent and a force of police swooped down upon Clare Island, and attempted to capture for arrears of rent the very wages John Bull fondly supposed he was paying to fill starving children's stomachs. How the trick is done is worth studying. The 'Loyal Minority' on the Mayo coast numbers only a few scores out of a couple of hundred thousand people ; but the few scores own all the land, possess all the castles and fair pastures, and fill all the offices of power and emolument. One of the chosen families is (let us say) X. By an arrangement worthy of our refined civilisation in its most inspired hour, X. the

Younger earns a handsome salary as poor-law inspector for administering public relief to the Clare Islanders, while X. the Elder (they are brothers) earns a double set of fees in appropriating for the landlord the fruit of the relief thus provided. X. the Elder, in fact, officiates both as Chancellor of the Exchequer and as Lord High Executioner. As sub-Sheriff of the county he wields all the powers and terrors of the law, and is accordingly sought after far and wide in the County Mayo as land-agent. He seeks the decree for possession as land-agent, and as Sheriff is in a position to command all the Queen's horses and all the Queen's men to execute it. Mr. Jackson admits he dislikes the patent double-acting apparatus, but professes that he can find no remedy for it. All the power of Britain is at hand to crush the starving peasant who boos a bailiff; but there is no power in the decrees of Venice to prevent the principal officer of the law from being principal officer of the landlord at the same time—from being, in short, according to the description in an old rhyme, ' Judge, jury, gallows, rope, and all.' Accordingly X. the Younger, having fulfilled his function as angel of charity on Clare Island, X. the Elder took the islanders in hand ; and X. the land-agent, having made his arrangements for pouncing upon the peasants' relief-wages and charity-grown potato-crops for rent, X. the Sheriff ordered a competent force of Queen's riflemen to his assistance to make straight his paths.

There ensued a six months' squalid and sickening war throughout the winter between peasant and landlord for the fruit of the miserable relief administered by the British taxpayer—a war in which the blows were all upon one side, for the poor Gaelic-speaking peasants had no weapon even of speech, while the landlord's raids were backed up with liberal musket blows, and with eighty Coercion prosecutions. I have had an opportunity recently of detailing to the House of Commons the incidents of last winter on Clare Island, and I do not propose to harrow your readers further with them here. The main point is that the myrmidons of the State actively assisted in robbing the poor-box they themselves had filled ; that the policemen, who a few months before visited the cabins as State almoners, revisited them now to spy out for the landlord's bailiff the peasant's mountain-goat or handful of potatoes ; that the very men and women who up to August had to be supported on the relief works were— eighty of them—prosecuted under the Coercion Act for ' illegal assembly' in collecting in their terror to watch the operations of the bailiff and riflemen ; that during a period of three stormy months they were no less than five times summoned to the mainland on the solemn charge of overawing the forces of the law, and once, in mere selfish cruelty, compelled to walk thirteen miles further inland in a snowstorm to convenience the Removable Magistrates ; and that, finally, the Removables from the Bench, and Mr. Jackson in the House of Commons, wound up the prosecutions with a lecture worthy of Mr. Podsnap in his most dithyrambic vein upon the benignity of British law and the glories of the British connection. The islanders, of course, only escaped from the Coercion Court to fall in the Eviction Court. At the last Castlebar Quarter Sessions, decrees for possession—which Mr. Gladstone well described as ' sentences of death '—were passed against nineteen island families ; X. the agent, with his decrees in his hand, moved X. the Sheriff for the usual quota of British bayonets to assert the clemency of the law. One family was evicted experimentally—as an

Irishman once directed a piper to play up ' " " The Boyne Water "—gently, to see could he stand it.'   If the British public ' can stand it ' [1] out will go the remaining eighteen families on the bleak island rocks, and out will go after them the remainder of the famishing islanders, for whom Mr. Balfour was only last year issuing pathetic appeals to British charity, and decking his policemen with angels' wings, and composing melting speeches in reply to his Removables' rhetoric.   And when the last of the O'Malleys are left roofless amidst the wild waves for not disgorging to the landlord the little store of food contributed for their starving children, surely they may well contrast piracy as practised on their island in the nineteenth century not altogether favourably with piracy as it was understood in the sixteenth.

But now comes the crowning touch of paternal government in Ireland.   For it turns out that while Mr. Balfour was spending tens of thousands of pounds out of public taxes in useless road-making, and keeping the island in an agony for the sake of a few hundred pounds of landlord's rents, Nature had all the time provided within gunshot of Clare Island a wealth of deep-sea fishing enough to have fed the islanders and paid the landlord fifty times over ; and that throughout three hundred years it never once occurred to a paternal Government that such a treasure was there, or to provide the islanders with the means of grasping it. Last week there were twenty-two steam trawlers in Clew Bay, gathering up tons of turbot, soles, and mackerel on every side of Clare Island—Scotch trawlers, English trawlers, Manx trawlers, even French trawlers—and not a single Irish boat in the lot.   For many years officials like

---

[1] The appeal to British public opinion stopped the evictions. They have never taken place since.

Sir Thomas Brady and the late Mr. J. A. Blake—men
with their hearts in their work, and who were consequently set down for cranks in the Black Book of Dublin
Castle, and doomed to retirement on the first pretext—
have been proclaiming in vain that a rich mine of deep-
sea fishing lay off the Western coasts if the people had
only seaworthy boats to work it. *Laissez-faire* answered
' Nonsense ! there is no fishing-bank off this cold coast
that would repay more ambitious gear than the ancient
spillet-hooks and hide-covered *currachs* of the natives.'
Accordingly to their spillets and canoes the natives were
left from famine-time to famine-time, while again and
again sums sufficient to have equipped great fishing-fleets
were poured out along the Mayo seaboard upon relief-
works as purposeless as the oakum picking or crank-
turning of a gaol-yard. It was left for some roaming
Frenchmen to plough their way to wealth along the coast
where an enlightened Dublin Castle could discern nought
but barrenness and food for Coercion. Those trawling-
steamers have made sad havoc of the poor islanders' rude
night-lines, and by the rattle of their paddles and their
voracious sweeping-brush style of fishing at the very mouth
of the bay, they have alarmed the fish and possibly done
permanent damage to the fishing ; but they have at least
proved that here, within stone-throw of the famishing
islanders, there is food and wealth exceeding relief funds a
thousand times over, and that the islanders can but lift
their empty hands in wonder while it is garnered by
strangers. There is a pathos too deep for words in one
fact mentioned to me last week by Father Molloy, the
true-hearted pastor of Clare Island. He was dependent
for his fish-dinner on Good Friday upon the courtesy of a
foreign trawler. His own luckless parishioners could but

watch from the shore while the strange steamers were loading up to the hatchways with turbot for the London or the Paris market. The strangers had fared so well that they charitably threw the coarser kinds of fish in their draw overboard to the natives!

Is it possible for human words to heighten the argument, either against eviction or against Dublin Castle government, preached by such facts? The last touch of gruesome comedy is given to the scene by the announcement that, while X. the Elder, with his evicting expedition, may any day again be descried off Clare Island, X. the Younger is being once more set in motion as poor-law inspector to report what is to be done, by emigration to Manitoba or otherwise, with the pestilent O'Malleys. If any Briton by his fireside likes to think the Irish difficulty is an affair of our grandfathers, or, at all events, of the days when the Balfourian bloom was on the rye, let him fix his eyes upon the thin figures of the O'Malleys, only too pitifully 'up to date,' on the Clare Island cliffs, wringing their helpless hands while a fleet of strange steamers carries off the treasures of the deep under their noses, and straining their eyes towards the point where any day the Sheriff's gunboat may loom in sight to evict them for rents less in moneys numbered than a French trawler might earn in a single cruise, and to cut off their last chance of sustenance by land or sea. Is it a contravention of the Coercion Act to sigh for one day of the lion-hearted old sea-queen who sleeps amidst the ocean surges under the ruins of the island abbey?

THE INFLUENCE OF THE IRISH LANGUAGE [1]

I am well aware of the difficulty of interesting an audience
of young Irishmen in the praises or fortunes of the Irish
language. It was not without considerable trepidation I
chose a topic so time-stricken for my address to a Society
whose work lies in the living present, and whose pathway
is strown with the promise of a golden future. There will
rise to impatient lips the demand, ' Do you seriously propose to make it a test of Irish Nationality that men shall
discard the language of Shakespeare and Burke, of Milton
and Newman, for the language of the cabins along a strip
of rock-bound Atlantic coast ? ' Nor will it be enough to
answer—' I should as soon propose to the world-spread
Irish race to surrender their hard-won inheritance on
the great English-speaking continents and coop themselves
up among the moors and rocks of Connaught.' ' Then
where is the use,' will be the triumphant demand of the
practical politician, ' in an age whose tendency it is to
substitute one universal language for all the languages of
Babel—where is the use of attempting to arrest the fate
of a dialect which is shorn of all modern graces, and
stunted of its natural growth since the Middle Ages, and
which, but for the outcries of a knot of musty enthusiasts,

[1] Lecture delivered May 13, 1892, before the Cork National Society,
of which the speaker is President.

is dying a natural death? Why trouble with vain voices from the past a nation which has its Parliament to win, its swamps to drain, its woollens to weave, and its fecund soil, longing to yield up a threefold increase of herds and yellow harvests?' To all of which I answer—First, that in the matter of languages, as in the matter of nationalities, side by side with the tendency to find a common bond of intercourse between races of men in those broad human concerns which make of all the world one country, there is a still more marked tendency in our time to cherish those distinguishing characteristics of blood, of language, and tradition, which constitute the individuality and stimulate the genius of nationalities, and which are to nations what domestic life is to individuals. A thousand people now-a-days have a smattering of more than one language for the one who could speak two languages a century ago. In the second place, while I should be the last to subtract any portion of the energies of the young men of Ireland from the conquest of a National Parliament, or from those great tasks of material and social regeneration which will come in its train, lost were the nation which should forget that the sacred passion of Nationality—which is the driving force and vital breath of all our struggles, the spell which makes hope enchanting, the consecration which lifts us above the paltry contentions of the hour, and makes even suffering and failure sweet—has its origin deep in the recesses of the past, among the old associations of which the Gaelic language is the very living voice and soul; and I cannot think that a society of young Corkmen who aspire to be the commissioned soldiers of Irish Nationality, will deem an hour altogether wasted in tracing a few of the particulars in which the Gaelic spirit has entered into the national character and must enter into any distinctively national literature, and in considering how comes the startling paradox that, with a generation of young Irishmen penetrated to the core with the passion of Irish Nationality, it should be necessary to brave the charge of tediousness to claim a kindly thought for that national language which is the oldest of our national possessions and the inalienable title-deed to the individuality of our race.

Of ancient monuments of other descriptions, which are, after all, only the stocks and stones of a dead past, we have come to think tenderly enough. Public indignation is now wide awake to the vandalism of the man who should cart away the delicate stone traceries of our old Cathedrals to build into his cabin walls, or turn the Royal cemeteries of the Boyne into quarries to mend roads withal. Every Irishman of finely-strung nature loves to piece together the stones of the cloisters of Cong, where the last High King of Ireland found a more durable than earthly kingdom. Our pulses quicken as we trace amidst the vestiges of the old town wall of Limerick the breach where King William's Brandenburg Regiment was blown into the air, and where Robert Dwyer Joyce's Blacksmith might have wielded his hammer. We follow Dr. Petrie's footsteps reverently among the mounds on Tara Hill, while he proves to us where stood the Mead-circling Hall, once glittering with the revelry of kings, and where the Chamber of Sunshine from whose windows of bright glass Grainne's soft eyes first lighted on her young Munster hero as he gained the goal from all the men of Leinster on the grassy plain. A broken column, a place-name, a mere mound glorified with the dust of heroes, may enable us to live over again the feasts, the royal jousts, the romances which lit up the land a thousand years ago. We have an archi-

E

tect of the Board of Works more or less (generally less) ready to patch up every crack and flaw that time works in our Round Towers and ruined Shrines. How comes it that alone among our national monuments the greatest and most venerable of them all is suffered to crumble to dust in our sight, with none but a few mournful watchers here and there to lament the stages of its doom? Of what avail, however, are tombs or battered ruins to enable us to realise, to touch, to feel the warm current of life revive in the veins of the picturesque generations who lived and loved and fought and feasted in this land before us, compared with the language which was the very voice of their souls—which was, in their own phrase, the pulse of their hearts—and which preserves for us, as in a national phonograph, the thoughts, the accents, the very inflections with which Oisin sang the songs of his youth, and King Brian cheered on his hosts, and Columbanus ruled half Western Europe from his cell in far-famed Bobbio?

Let us take another aspect in which the national language is the national treasure-house. It is the unique distinction of the Gaelic race that the lowliest family inherits a genealogy as well authenticated and as rich in inspiring traditions as the family tree of most modern dukes. For the last three centuries, indeed, the record is blurred or defaced. The sharp facts of the Celtic genealogies, verified every three years in the great national assemblies, and stamped indelibly in the national memory by the bards and shanachies, merge into one vast, indistinguishable scene of degradation for the race. But now that the race has risen to its feet, and can look back behind the weltering gulf of the past three hundred years, we can take up the distant traces of whence we came, and, by evidences as reliable as those which attest any of the facts of

human history, we can follow back the fortunes of every
great Celtic family, through the varied scenery of our
island story, until it is lost in the romantic mists which
float about the yellow-haired Milesians landing in Kerry
in days before Athens won her violet crown—in days,
perhaps, when the towers of Ilium were still standing.
Nor is there in this sense of national good breeding aught
that could affront the most democratic claim of equality
for all the sons of men.   There are few or none of us who
can trace that unbroken line of ancestors which is the envy
of modern vulgarians.   The peculiar prerogative of our
race is that, while it has been purified by centuries of
equality in obscure poverty, and braced by the most
copious and diversified mixture of blood, it has been at the
same time preserved, with all its energies and aspirations,
intact, for a *renaissance* in which it has all that heralds
can rake from the most aristocratic lineage to elevate and
ennoble men's ambitions—all that is comprehended in the
descent from a nation of heroes, and the consecrative
stamp of a nation of saints.   And we have this further
safeguard against mere pride of birth in the tuft-hunting
sense of the term—that while the confusion of the last
three centuries has left little or nothing to distinguish the
child of the chief from the child of the lowliest clansman,
the course of our history gives to the Irish poor the consolation of thinking that the more complete their present
poverty, the more probably it was earned by some heroic
ancestor who preferred a bold dash for liberty against
Carew or Cromwell to broad lands and apostate English
titles.

   This is no inconsiderable heritage for a nation.   Fancy
a dumb yokel in the fens of Lincolnshire being able to pick
out his progenitor among the squadrons at the battle of

Hastings as proudly as any Howard or De Winton of them all. It is not too much to claim that, in spite of wave after wave of confiscation and seeming extinction, hundreds of Irish clans still hover indomitably around their old tribal territories, who, beginning where the ancestry of the modern Irish aristocracy ends, can claim descent from a line of forefathers as well established historically as that of the English Royal house, and extending back in princely array to days when the Roman eagles were still fluttering over captive Europe. The Irish race, while it marches abreast, if not in advance, of democratic progress in these countries and in the United States, has its blood ennobled at the same time with the influence of all that is most venerable and chivalrous in the antique world. The Gaelic language is as it were our muniment of title to this ancient royal inheritance. The Gaelic genealogies, like those of MacFirbis, many of them to this day buried in undeciphered rotting manuscripts, supply us with an unrivalled National portrait gallery, in which all the great branches of the race of Eochy or the race of Conn can behold not only the kings and warriors of their line, but the tribal harpers, the tribal physicians, tribal judges and romancists, and cup-bearers and carvers. Yet, like Charles Surface in a flippant spendthrift hour, the Irish nation sells its inestimable gallery of ancestors for a song, without even the regretful sigh which the graceless prodigal of Sheridan's play expended upon the family portraits. The result is not merely to cut us off from an heroic Celtic world—as bright as the pages of Scott and more authentic than those of Herodotus—but to make Irish Nationality an affair of yesterday, an invention of the last English-speaking hundred years, and to surrender those higher landmarks and title-deeds of national individuality which we derive from laws and institutions, and modes of thought all but as ancient and unalterable as the ocean cliffs that secure our Island's throne of nationhood amidst the seas.   Our stock of political ideas dates from Lucas or Wolfe Tone in the latter end of the last century.   Our literature is composed in the main of the songs and essays of Young Ireland.   Far be it from me to suggest that the young Irish mind could be drilled in a better school of manly persistency than in Wolfe Tone's, or moulded to nobler purposes than under the glowing influence of Thomas Davis.   It is outside my present aim to discuss how much more than slavish imitation or barren criticism of the Young Ireland writers is needed if ever the rich Indies of national literature, which Davis rather coasted than had time to explore, are to yield up their treasures.   All I desire to be marked for the moment is that the peculiar glow and charm which have enabled Thomas Davis to acquire an empire over the Irish youth of the present generation even more powerful than over his own—the temperament swept by ever-shifting mystic lights and shadows, now bathed in a lover's tenderness, now flashing with the delight of battle, or joyous as a wine-cup at a feast of old—were derived from a passionate attachment to the old Gaelic tongue, and a sympathetic nature saturated with the wild sensitive spiritual traditions which the old Gaelic literature exhales as naturally as an Irish meadow exhales perfumes on a May morning. No man who understood only the English language could ever have written the 'Lament for Owen Roe O'Neill,' or (to cite another master of the Celtic lyre) 'The Wail for the Earls.'   Nor can it be other than a confounding reflection that in the mysterious intellectual commerce of the living and the dead, the Irish Nationalist of our day

would be as a man that heareth not in the Parliament of
Tara ; he would listen to O'Neill's address to his army and
understand not a word; he would find himself an alien
even around the camp-fires of Mountcashel's Brigades ;
and that, on the other hand, if Cuchullin and Finn, if
King Niall and King Brian, if St. Columbkille and St.
Colman, if Art McMurrough, and Feach O'Byrne, and
Red Hugh O'Donnell—if the men whose holiness has made
the Irish earth holy, or whose deeds by field and flood live
in the very life-blood of Irish Nationality—could but
visibly revisit the many-streamed hills of Erin, they would
have to shrink back among the huts along the western
rocks in order to make themselves understood, or, possibly,
in order not to be laughed at.

The reasons which men give for the uneasy shudder
with which they listen to enthusiasts for the preservation
of the Gaelic Language may be summed up in this, that it
is a language hard to learn and useless when learned.
There is nothing to be gained by shirking the fact that it
is at first sight a language apt to be the despair of
beginners. The Greek or Latin grammar, once mastered,
admits you into a wide branching palace wherein the
modern Romance languages are only so many different
apartments filled with familiar acquaintances, clothed in
an ever-brightening dress, and murmuring ever-softer
accents. The Gaelic, on the contrary, stands apart in
sturdy independence, girt with a stormy Irish sea, true to
the root-words of the first century in the nineteenth,
proudly maintaining a mode of notation peculiarly its own,
whose function it seems to be to wage a perpetual civil
war against the consonants, and rich in wholly strange and
unaccustomed sounds as different from the mincing charms
of French or Italian pronunciation as an Irish lullaby is

from the tipsy music of ' La Fille de Madame Angot.'
One is prone to repine at the want of distinction in the
tense-ending of the verbs, to grow dizzy over the difference between the spelling of words and their pronunciation, and to storm at the long litanies of compounded
pronouns and prepositions.   The tongue aches at the first
endeavours to pronounce words which seem mere dis-
orderly mobs of consonants. Even after the rules enlighten
you as to how eclipsing letters soften the asperities of
those unruly c's and b's and t's, and how the aspiration
dots knock them summarily on the head, you sometimes
grow as nervous lest no consonant at all should survive to
take a firm hold of, as you were at first pained for the fate
of the vowels.   But in all this the difficulties are more
apparent than real.   To my mind the one formidable
difficulty of the Irish language is the pronunciation. Until
the pronunciation dawns upon a beginner all is chaos and
barrenness.   The pronunciation once learned, as it can
only be from Irish lips, the rest becomes order, harmony,
and a labour of love.

I may be permitted to cite my own case as containing
balm for the discouraged.   More than twenty years ago
I so far mastered the grammar rules and dry bones of
the language for myself that, with the help of ' O'Brien's
Dictionary,' which I found in the library of the Cork
Queen's College, I could stumble through an old Irish
Chronicle with rather more than the facility with which a
schoolboy stumbles through Livy's Histories.   But it was
with even less relish.   Try as I did ever so hard to educe
music out of this provoking hurly-burly of words, no
written rules could serve me.   I knew there must be
hidden somewhere the spirit melody in which generations
of Irish scholars found raptures ;   but the rapture was not

for me. I knew the language, but I knew it as a man who raises the lid of a coffin knows the once living man inside. Last year the fate which brought me within the walls of Galway Gaol brought me also into occasional communion with a chaplain, to whom the Gaelic accents came as naturally as mountain air to his lungs. For the first time the dead language my eyes had ached over, like the field of bones seen in the prophet's vision, began to stir with life and to be clad with beauty. The lawless consonants which seemed to defy articulate utterance rushed from the lips like streams from the hills, or clans to the battle. The charm was wound up. The language as it first looked in books was as different from the language clothed in the rich soft sunshine of the native pronunciation as the heather mountain over which one gropes and flounders in the dark differs from the same heather mountain sparkling with the amethyst lights of the morning sun. I have no pretension to more than a sort of tourist acquaintance with the Gaelic world, but it may cheer those who are even less versed in the language than myself to know that the little I did learn proved to be an unfailing refuge from heart-breaking political cares, and an acquirement which I esteem decidedly cheap at the price of six months' imprisonment. Let me offer one further suggestion for the benefit of learners. If they would kindle within themselves at once a living interest in the language, let them not begin even with so attractive a piece of mediæval Gaelic as 'The Pursuit of Diarmid and Grainne,' for they will be disheartened by finding its pages crowded with words unintelligible to the Gaelic-speaking peasant. A foreigner commencing to learn English would soon give it over in despair if he tried his English acquaintance with the language of Chaucer, or even with the language of

Shakespeare; and most of the old Irish romances date as far back as Chaucer or earlier. Let them rather begin with Dr. Douglas Hyde's fascinating leabar Sgeulaigeacta, which places you at once in sympathy with the living Gaelic world around you, which catches the spirit of the spoken language with humour, with sim- plicity, and with a helpful sprinkling of more or less familiar Anglo-Irishisms, and, as it were, welcomes the new-comer without ceremony to a corner beside an old Irish fireside where the good old fairy hosts, and the one- eyed giants, and beautiful princesses of our childhood rise up merrily out of the comfortable winter blaze. To acquire such proficiency in the Gaelic language as would create the desire to learn more, demands no greater labour than is required to learn French, or to learn the fiddle, or to learn swimming, or to master any of the other accomplish- ments in which quite naturally and properly our Irish youth never grudge to expend time and enthusiasm.

The question remains: Is the acquirement of our ancient mother-tongue—the tongue of bards and chiefs, of piety and love and war, which shines upon us through- out our ages of glory, which remained with us through the centuries of our unspeakable captivity—worth even this modest exertion in the eyes of a young Irish Nationalist? The very question imports a reproach from which none of us can altogether escape. To know that one of the best approaches to an Irish dictionary is a translation from the German; that famous French and German scholars find in our despised tongue priceless intimations as to the early history of languages and races, and law codes as rich in interest for the student of human institutions as the Pandects of Justinian; that the antiquarians of Scotland or Wales or Brittany would give their eyes for written

records such as those which are packed away unregarded
in the chests of Trinity College and the Royal Irish
Academy—all this may surely excuse the outcries of
Gaelic enthusiasts against the fashion of dismissing the
venerable Gaelic learning in its own land as a peasant's
jargon or a pack of gibberish about Finn McCool. But it
will be said: 'This is an argument addressed to learned
bodies, not to the common people. Doubtless Irish Universities and academies ought to give us a little more
original Irish science — sociological, philological, and
archæological—even if they had to fill their Books of
Transactions with a little less general science at second-
hand. You cannot expect a general public to rummage
old manuscripts of the twelfth century or puzzle over
obsolete legal dialects to which no more than half-a-dozen
scholars in a generation can find the key. The mass of
men, after all, want to be amused, not to be set tasks. Is
there aught in your vaunted Gaelic literature as full of
vivid human interest as a play of Ben Jonson, or even
that would enable the average reader in a public library
to pass as enjoyable a leisure hour as a novel of Fielding
or Thackeray?' To this I venture to return a confident
affirmative. Those who decry Gaelic literature are those
who are ignorant of it. I have yet to meet a man once
practically acquainted with the language who dropped it
for want of literary material to feed upon. It is quite true
that there is no modern Gaelic literature to compare with
that which sprang up in Italy in the courts of the Medici
or the d'Este, or in England in the splendid times of
Elizabeth and Anne, or in France under the smiles of the
Grand Monarch. The men who might have been the
Petrarchs or the Molières or the Ben Jonsons of the Gael
had darker cares to occupy them during the last seven

hundred years than polishing their metres, or dipping
their language in the Pactolian stream of the great classi-
cal revival.   Strip English literature of nine-tenths of the
poetry, of the plays, of the histories and philosophies,
accumulated since the days of Piers Plowman, and con-
fide the care of the English language for all those centuries
to a band of hunted peasants in the wilds of Cornwall, and
you will only have applied to English letters the conditions
upon which any Gaelic literature at all has come down to
us.   On the other hand, reverse the fate of the Gaelic
Muse, which in centuries when the darkness of a brutish
night overspread the intellect of Europe had already
imagined the graceful scenery of the Land of Youth and
the exquisite chivalry of the fight between Cuchullin and
Ferdiad—suppose that the courts of Irish kings could have
continued to shower their favours upon the masters of
song and learning—suppose the Italian models from which
the Elizabethan dramatists borrowed, or the mighty French
masters who coloured the literature of Queen Anne, had
presented themselves on the Irish poet's bower in place of
statutes rewarding the slaying of Irish harpers on a more
liberal scale than Irish wolves—suppose that a long
dynasty of Goldsmiths, Swifts, Berkeleys, Burkes, Sheri-
dans, Currans, and Moores had given to Gaelic letters the
wealth of philosophy, imagination, and eloquence they
have squandered upon a stepmother English tongue—
who can measure to what a degree of expansion the
language of Oisin might have attained in the nineteenth
century ?   A couple of centuries of the Goths and Huns
were enough to debase the proud literature of Rome. There
are only three centuries accounted the Dark Ages.   Yet,
when they were over, civilisation had to begin all over
again, as after Noah's flood.   Ten centuries of confusion,

for three of which the Danes are answerable, and for the rest the successors of Strongbow, have weighed upon the Gaelic intellect since the days of our native universities ; yet there has survived to us from the wreckage of our ten dark ages a body of laws, of records, of arts and sciences and romances, for which, so far as I know, there is no rival to be found in any contemporary nation, even within the sphere of Roman culture. In the Brehon law tracts alone—in the singularly attractive, though faulty, tribal system which bound the population of a whole territory into one family—in the laws of hospitality and of poor relief—in the ancient Celtic land system, so permeated with what is best in modern theories of Christian socialism, so very much more ingenious than the modern doctrine of dual ownership—in the study of the manners of the ancient Irish alone—their homes, and food, and pastimes—there is material more fascinating, even for a lazy reader, than in a modern book of travel.

Nor need even the most insatiable seeker after the fiction of the circulating libraries turn away unsatisfied. Side by side with historical records which no European scholar will now dispute, we have tales, voyages, court-ships, and hairbreadth adventures, even yet unpublished, sufficient, it is estimated, to cover more than twenty thou-sand quarto pages of print—tales of magic, tales of chivalry, tales of love, and, I am sorry to say, not always true love. The very blemishes of the Gaelic romance have their charm of rugged truth-telling. The three-volume novel reader would like to close the story of Grainne with some deed of sublime vengeance for the murder of her hero. We resent the notion of her being won over to wed his elderly murderer. But such triumphs of masculine insistence there be, as witness the crooked King Richard's conquering the hand of the Lady Anne in a single scene; and the Celtic dramaturgist proceeds to tell the truth and shame the devil, and rings down the curtain with a chorus of contemptuous laughter from the warriors. Woman's constancy, on the other hand, is vindicated in the soft, clinging affection, stronger than death, of Deirdre for her lost Naisi ; and for the matter of friendship between man and man—the friendship that loves with all but a woman's softness, yet smites with the dutiful valour of a hero—I know of no episode in human history, not even the history of David and Jonathan, more beautiful, more touching, or more true than that of Cuchullin's fight with the comrade of his boyhood at the Ford of Ardee.

One of the standing reproaches against our race is that the Celtic imagination has never invented an Epic. No more ignorant charge could be selected, even out of the litany of calumnies which insolent conquerors appended to the Irish name. The Gaelic genius had brought forth two great Epics—that which gathers around Queen Maev's name, and that which gathers around the name of Finn—centuries before any of the modern Romance languages had produced anything better than a village rhyme. It is true, we cannot point out our particular Homer or Dante turning out an immortal poem complete in all its parts, and transmitting it to us in a faultless Elzevir edition, with a portrait of the author. For Oisin, indeed, as the creator of Fenian romance, we have as good historical evidence as we have for Homer as the composer of all the ballads of the ' Iliad '; but the man or men who sang the glories of the Red Branch Knights are lost to us in the twilight, all but as utterly as the men who built the tumulus of Dowth, or who set up the Cromlechs. But that such men there were in ancient Erin, not merely

as single stars, but in constellations ; that the order of
poets was for generations as powerful as the order of
kings, and sometimes more powerful ; and that, as the
intellectual legacy of that order, we inherit two bodies of
epic poetry, permeated by a worship of beauty, a pity
for the weak, a contempt for cowardice and cunning, a
joyous strength and valour, as ennobling as inspired the
songs of Troy, and, at the same time, a native tenderness,
heartiness, and simplicity as distinctively homelike as the
note of a blackbird in an Irish glen—all this a race of
laborious and unrequited Irish scholars have now placed
it beyond the power of flippancy or malice to contest.
' The Pursuit of Diarmid and Grainne,' even in its present
version, dates from the eleventh century—that is to say,
from a time when there was not yet a single written
document in the Italian language, and a century before
the tales of Spanish chivalry were yet invented. It is certain that the earliest of our existing manuscripts were
only transcripts of tales told, and probably written down,
many centuries before. To look for a troubadour's word-
carving, or for Grecian graces of style in narrative thus
jotted down by unknown scribes from unknown story-
tellers' lips, would be like expecting Tennyson's mellow
metres from an Anglo-Saxon rhymer.

The value of the Gaelic literature lies in its spirit, not
in its letter. Its value in the loveless old age of the
nineteenth century is greater than, perhaps, even the most
ardent protesters against the extinction of the Gaelic language suspect. The world is a-weary with pessimism. It
has lost its innocence. It is losing its faith in most things
here or hereafter. Whatever portion of its energies is not
given to the pitiless rush for wealth, or self-advertisement,
or material luxury, is spent in morbidly analysing its own

ailments of body or mind. For this poison of moral and
intellectual despair which is creeping through a sad world's
veins, what cheerier antidote is within reach than the living
tide of health, and hope, and simplicity, and hilarity, the
breezy objectiveness and stoutness of muscle, and ardour of
emotion, which flows full and warm through the heroic
myths of the men of Erin ?   If the world is content to
go as far as Norway for a new proof of how wicked and
unhappy human nature can make itself, why not also go
to Ireland to hunt the wild woods of Ben Gulban with
Finn's mighty men, to see the golden towers of the Tir
Tairngire glittering on the western wave, to participate in
the glorious carouse of the ¡Fair of Carmán, or to live
again the charmed life of the post-Christian days, when
the vesper bells of saints sang the quiet valleys to their
rest, and the welcome of kings laughed merrily out upon
the stranger in the night ?

The Celtic spirit is the saving salt of a materialistic
age.   Celtic hearts in our own days have carried the fire
of divine faith into the depths of the New World as
bright as the night it was kindled by Patrick on the Hill
of Slane. As with the supernatural, so with the intellectual ideals, sympathies, blemishes, and virtues of the
race. They retain their pristine sincerity and their in-
communicable glow. Now, if there is anything clearer
than that Celtic ideals do not find satisfaction in the
English tongue—that they, so to say, feel an alien chill
and discomfort in their English garb—it is that they, on
the contrary, experience a feeling of kinship in the Irish
language and in the old Irish lore, such as a man might
experience at sight of the turf smoke curling out of his
native cabin by some fairy-haunted Irish rath after wan-
dering among the splendours of foreign cities. If there

is such a thing as ' the well of English undefiled' whence
whatever is best in English literature is drawn, still more
is there a holy well of uncontaminated Gaelic from which
any distinctively national literature will have to derive its
inspiration.   Davis, and Mangan, and Ferguson are great
in proportion as they caught the Gaelic glow, and Moore
failed in so far as he was a stranger to it.   Not in Russia,
not in Norway, not in the outworn East, may the world
find any permanent refreshment for its jaded spirit, but by
the old Gaelic firesides, in the hunting booths of Diarmid
and Oscar, in the cells of Colman and Brendan amidst the
ocean's dirges, in the riches buried amidst the ruins of
Gaelic civilisation, like a fairy crock of gold under some
haunted castle ; and whoso shall have the magic gift of
discovering the treasure to the world's eyes will do so not
by slavishly copying the old Gaelic forms of dead things,
but by importing into the actual life of the world around
us the blithesomeness, healthfulness, and simple-hearted-
ness, the ardour in love, and the relish in war, the full-
bodied enjoyment of this pleasant green world, the wild
pathos of its night-side, and the thrilling faith in the
mystic encompassing spirit-world beyond, which give to
antique Gaelic literature its charm, and to the Gaelic race
its indestructible vitality.

But it will be said, why wring our hands over the
inevitable ?   The god Pan is dead.   The speakers of the
Irish language are dying off by tens of thousands
every decade ; not many more tens of thousands remain
to die off.   What rational hope can there be of retaining,
as a living tongue at least, a language in such extremities ?   In the first place, the Irish language is not in the
direful extremities which are sometimes taken for granted.
Drawing a line from north to south through the centre of
the island, roughly speaking, one half of the population

on the western side of the line still understand Irish, and
hundreds of thousands who do not understand it unconsciously employ many of its peculiarities in their English
speech, and speak with an accent peculiarly adaptable to
the rich, liquid ꝑlᴀċᴀiꞃᴀꝉl enunciation of the Gael.   According to the late census returns 307,000 persons still
understand Irish in the province of Munster, and 119,000
in this county of Cork alone.   In addition, a million at
least of our Gaelic colonists in the Highlands and Islands
of Scotland still speak the old mother-tongue with rather
less difference of pronunciation than there is between the
common speech of London and the common speech of
Lancashire.   That is to say, the Gaelic is still the living
language of more people than speak any one of half-a
dozen national languages in Europe, which are, nevertheless, flourishing, and likely to flourish—Romaic, Greek,
and Servian, and Bulgarian and Norwegian, and Danish
and Welsh.   The truth is the Irish language is dying, not
of inanition, but of the fashion, and as a fashion mutable
is the decree for its extinction.   Bitter things have been
said of those who in the last fifty years were used to chide
Irish schoolchildren caught lapsing into their own mother-
tongue ; and no doubt it was a sorry spectacle.   But it
was emigration, not the ferule of the old pedants, that
drove the Irish language out of fashion.   Once the eyes
of the Irish peasants were directed to a career in the golden
English-speaking continents beyond the setting sun, their
own instincts of self-preservation, even more than the exhortation of those responsible for their future, pointed to
the English language as no less essential than a ship to
sail in and a passage ticket to enable them to embark on
it, as a passport from their miserable surroundings to
lands of plenty and independence beyond the billows.

F

And any attempt to revive the Irish language on the basis of cutting off any section of the Irish population from the equipment of the English language in the battle of life would be, in my judgment, as futile as it would be inhuman. But in the first place the purely Irish-speaking districts are precisely those from which our present educational system banishes any effective knowledge of the English language by insisting upon teaching it, not in the language which the pupils understand, but in the very foreign language the rudiments of which they have yet to learn, and which is thus presented to them in a shape that is unintelligible, discouraging, and repulsive. It is as if you proposed to grind the Greek verbs into the head of an English child by talking Homer at him. All that the Gaelic-speaking child is really taught is an unjust and paralysing sense of his own inferiority and stupidity. But the cardinal error of the foes of the Gaelic language is that a smattering of English is the beginning and end of wisdom for an Irish peasant. The true decisive factor in this problem is not the shamefully-treated youth of the Irish-speaking seaboard, who are deliberately prevented from learning either Gaelic or English effectively for fear they would prefer Gaelic, but it is the far more numerous section of the population who understand both Irish and English. In the county of Kerry, for example, according to the census returns just published, while the number of persons who speak Irish alone is 4,481, there are no less than 69,700 out of a total population of 179,000 who speak both Irish and English. It is this bilingual population by which the possible future of the Irish language is to be gauged. Who will deny that their intelligence, far from being cramped, is strengthened and diversified by a knowledge of the two languages ? They experience no more conflict between the two than between a knowledge of the multiplication table and a knowledge of the Catechism. While they find the English tongue as indispensable as English coin in the commerce of men, they find in the Gaelic language also, in the more sacred home-life of an Irish community, treasures of devotion and affection, a balm for bruised hearts, a music of old times, a smack of rotund hospitality, a vehicle of fireside talk and of patriotic inspiration, and of young love whisperings under the milk-white thorn on the May eves, such as no Irish heart will ever find in equal luxuriance in the chilly English speech.

In that direction, so far as I can see, lies an assured future for the Irish language. The battle for its preservation will be won upon the day when the half-million of people who still understand the language are made to feel that a knowledge of Irish is not an encumbrance or a reproach, but an accomplishment to be proud of, to be envied for, and to be transmitted to their children as religiously as old family silver.

Let me give you two examples from my own experience of how grievously mere fashion operates to the contrary at this moment. A youngster whom I met on Croaghpatrick last autumn mentioned to me that when the Rosary was recited in his father's cabin every night the old people gave out the first part of the prayer in the ancient tongue and the children made the responses in English. The case presented, I think, a graphic and most moving picture both of the process of decay of the old tongue and of the ease with which that process might even yet be arrested. Who can doubt that if the children were taught to consider it a patriotic feather in their caps, and not a badge of inferiority, to be able to answer the old folk in their own tongue, they would quickly discard their muddled English for limpid Irish, and find comfort as well as fervour in the exchange? My second experience was even more striking. A great prelate of distinguished attainments in Irish was on his way to the visitation of a parish where almost everybody understood that language. I asked should we have the advantage of hearing him address the people in Irish? The answer was that nothing would give him greater pleasure—that the native tongue alone could sound all the depths of devotion in the Irish heart, but that one could not insult an Irish-speaking congregation more effectively than by addressing them in Irish—that they would take it as a suggestion that they were a pack of barbarians who knew no English.

We have no right to be too hard upon such a senti- ment. It is not surprising that the simple-hearted peasants of the West should have come to think so meanly of the dialect of their own smoky cabins, associated as it is in their minds with every tradition of poverty and ignorance and lurking shame, in comparison with the proud con- quering language of England, the language of the schools and of the courts and of the great, clothed in the beauty of an unsurpassable literature, supported by the power of innumerable bayonets, and carrying the key to the king- doms of the earth in its hand. But here again we have to deal not with the enlightened judgment of a people, but with the prejudice of a twilight state of mind, with a fashion rather than with a natural necessity. The Western village populations have only to learn that in the most favoured parts of Ireland the Gaelic language is as much honoured and cultivated as it has hitherto been despised ; that young Irishmen in the Irish cities are engaged in acquiring it as ardently as all young fellows of intelligence

at present acquire French ; that strangers from other parts
of Ireland make pilgrimages to the Irish-speaking districts
as to the holy wells of the old Irish speech, and find its
accents as they rush from the peasants' lips possessed of
as strong a charm as the breeze upon the mountain crags
or the organ voice of the ocean swelling through the caves
of Achill or Clare Island ; and the shrewd western moun-
taineer will soon learn to think better of his language
and himself.   Make him feel by all means that English
is and must continue to be the language of intercourse
with the outer world—one of the first necessaries of life to
his boys and girls in the English harvest fields or the
mighty American cities.   Let him only learn that there is
no disgrace, but, on the contrary, honour and privilege, in
yielding to the natural instinct which tells him that his
heart throbs with holier and more tender emotions when
the pulpit speaks the language of the old saints, and that
his winter fireside is all the purer and brighter when it is
warmed again with the play of the old Gaelic fancy, and
when the deadly taciturnity which the cold English has
cast over the Irish cabin dissolves under the spell of the
rich accents which were as the distilled honey at the feasts
of the hospitable Gael.   Once make it clear to those who
still know Irish that they possess an enviable gift, one as
pleasant and invigorating to the Celtic soul as the game of
hurling is to the Celtic thews and sinews, and you have
established a firm security against the extinction of the
language.

But that is not enough.   If the more cultivated masses
of the Irish people want the Gaelic-speaking peasantry
to adopt a fashion, they must themselves set the fashion.
The man who would either decry or laud the Gaelic
language must first learn it.   It is not for me, in observa-

tions merely meant to set young Irishmen thinking, to attempt to lay down the limits within which a revival of the Irish language may be practicable. We should be but copying the precedents observed in Wales and in the Scottish Highlands if, in any parish where a fourth or more of the school-goers spoke Gaelic, a Gaelic-speaking schoolmaster, specially well paid for his bilingual accomplishments, were to be appointed, and if in every Gaelic-speaking petty sessions district a knowledge of the native tongue were to be made a prime qualification for magistrates and public officials within its borders.

Going a step higher, there seems to be no good reason, either of utility or of culture, why the national language should not take the place of Latin and Greek, or even of French, in our intermediate courses. For nine out of every ten young heads crammed with bad Latin and worse French, these attainments vanish almost with the publication of the prize list, while a knowledge of the language which would open to them the hearts of the Gaelic peasantry, and the secrets of their forefathers' romantic story, would remain with them a source of living intellectual interest. No less than 403 candidates in Gaelic presented themselves to the Intermediate examiners last year. Inasmuch as probably a couple of hundred thousand of our young countrymen have been condemned to nibble at French and Latin, here would be a sacred band enrolled at once to snatch up the torch of Gaelic lore from the western turf fires and carry it burning merrily through the Island. The Irish Catholic Episcopacy have opened the way to a still vaster change by erecting a Professorship of Irish in Maynooth. It is not an exaggeration to say that if the Rev. Professor O'Growney could only impart his own enthusiasm to the young priests who quit Maynooth in

any single year, it would be as impossible to uproot from
the Irish soil the language in which Oisin sang as to
uproot the faith which St. Patrick planted. But what
seems to me more needful than all else for the permanent
revival and development of the language is some such
modification of the existing Irish Academy, or creation of
a new one, as might gather together the force of Celtic
intellect into a body not content to sink into the indolence
of a club, not so languid of spirit as to surrender to a
South Kensington collection of curiosities the inestimable
relics of Celtic antiquity bequeathed to them by the pious
patriotism of generations of Hudsons, Hardimans, and
Wildes ; but a body learned enough to be law-givers of
the language, fond enough to bestow upon it enthusiasm
and affection, and sufficiently broad-minded to surround it
with all those charms of poetic, historic, and archæological
associations which would appeal to every cultivated mind
in the country. Such an Academy, combining (if one
may illustrate by living types) the conscientious erudition
of Mr. Gilbert, in a cognate subject, with something of
Dr. Haughton's light magnetic touch, and Dr. Douglas
Hyde's enthusiastic cultivation of the living Gaelic, would
bring provincialisms to an authoritative standard, would
prune the language of its decayed consonants, purify the
style of the slovenly copyists and story-tellers according to
modern canons of variety and elegance, and create a new
national literature—whether in the Gaelic tongue or the
English—enriched with the genius, warmth, sincerity,
and quaint mountain charm of the old. Nor need its
mission stop here. There would be the broken chords of
the world-dispersed Irish race to be taken up and attuned ;
there would be all the gracious accessories of national life
to blossom again in its sunshine—the re-awakening of

Irish music, the painting of the tender Irish landscapes, and the all but unknown art of drawing a genuine Irish peasant, the rehabilitation of a national drama, the amassing of priceless Irish historical material now being consumed by the moths in English libraries or foreign monasteries; the making the evening valleys ring again with the innocent glee of the Kerry dance, and the plains of Tara with the shouts of the ancient festivals and pastimes. Is it even too bold a vision of far-off years to dream of a time when, passing the stormy Moyle once more into the Scottish isles and glens, the children of the Irish Gael might draw closer even than recent events have drawn those bonds of blood and clanship which once bound us to our Scottish soldier colonists who conquered with Angus and knelt to Columbkille?—nay, spreading still further a-field and a-main, discover new nations of blood relations in our near cousins of the Isle of Man and our farther cousins among the misty mountains of Wales and the old-world cities of Brittany; and combining their traditions, their aspirations, and genius with the ever-growing Celtic element with which we have penetrated the New World, confront the Giant Despair which is preying upon this aged century, body and soul, with a world-wide Celtic league, with faith and wit as spiritual, with valour as dauntless, and sensibilities as unspoilt as when all the world and love were young?

I do not ask my countrymen to withdraw their eyes from nearer and more vital objects to fix them on these distant visions; but I do respectfully ask them to dismiss the ignoble thought that the ambition to preserve our national language belongs to the region of crotchets or of boredom, and to recognise that among all the forms of national efflorescence which an Irish Parliament will bring into life, the popularisation of the old musical speech of the Gaels will be one of the easiest of accomplishment as well as one of the pleasantest duties of national piety. The story of the belief in, and the clinging to, the Gaelic language is in itself a romance pathetic enough for tears. Age after age, while the native tongue was a badge of contempt, a passport to persecution, even a death warrant—the schools suppressed, the printing press unknown, the relics of the national literature scattered in mouldering manuscripts, secreted as the damning evidences of superstition or treason—there were always to be found the poet, the scholar, the ecclesiastic, to foster the sacred fire, the outlawed treasure of the Gael, in his bosom—to suffer, and hunger, and die for its sake. In the days of Elizabeth it was Duald MacFirbis, dedicating his great Genealogy to his ruined Celtic Prince with the pathetic lament that no Irish prince any longer owned enough of territory to afford himself a grave. Or it was Michael O'Clery, one of the Four Masters, in his poor Franciscan cell, ' transcribing every old material that his eager hand could reach,' for it seemed to him, in his own quaint words, ' a cause of pity and grief, for the glory of God and the honour of Erin, how much the race of Gael, the son of Niall, had gone under a cloud of darkness.'

The centuries pass. The soil of Ireland is confiscated anew after the Cromwellian wars, and confiscated all over again after the Williamite wars. The last relics of the old Celtic civilisation seem to shrink into the very earth before the laws and dripping sword of England. And still in Keating's cave in Aherlow Glen, and O'Flaherty's cabin in Connemara, and Lynch's cell in Louvain, the undying spark is kept alive, and the treasonous manuscripts of the Gael are cherished for happier days. Not happier, but more unhappy days arrive. A century of humiliation compared to which the Drogheda massacre was glory, and the lost battle of the Boyne inspiring—the century of the diabolical Penal Laws of Anne and the First Georges—broods over the Celtic race. The Gaelic schoolmaster becomes a legal abomination. The schoolhouse, as well as the Masshouse, cowers in a lonely glen under the rains and storms. Still will not the imperishable spirit of Gaelic song and scholarship consent to give up the ghost. In the very dead of night of the eighteenth century burst out the songs of Carolan, amazing as the notes of a nightingale in mid-winter; and then were heard ' The Blackbirds ; ' and the Ɔᴘᴊᴍᴊᴎ Ꝺoᴎᴎ Ꝺílᴊᴦ and the ' Dawning of the Day ' of the Munster Bards—that mysterious band of minstrels who started up here, there, and everywhere, for no other reason than that the overcharged Irish heart had either to sing or die—a Charleville farmer, a schoolmaster in Clare, a blind musician in Tipperary—men whose names even are unknown to the people who still find in their songs the heavenly nutriment of their sweetest emotions and of their most passionate hours.

Then came the period when patriots and scholars, sprung from the ruling blood and speaking the Saxon speech, began to realise dimly the charms of national archæology, and of the venerable Gaelic literature that had been so long hunted on the hills and ridiculed in the schools—the period when the great Edmund Burke was the means of securing for Trinity College the manuscript of the priceless Brehon Law Code after its century of wanderings, neglect and decay in the cabins of Tipperary ; when O'Flaherty's *Ogygia* was purchased for twenty guineas, and the great compilation of the leᴀbᴀᴘ Ᏸᴘeᴀc for 3*l.* 13*s.* 8*d.* ; the period of the pathetic scene in the history of an apparently lost tongue, when the Seṅċur ṁóp, recovered as by a miracle from the proscriptions and neglect of ages, was found to be written in a dialect, which was no longer intelligible to the most learned Irish scholar then alive. Finally, there came the discovery of the great French and German philologists, that the Gaelic language afforded as inestimable a key to the history of pre-Roman Europe as the baths of Caracalla and the golden house of the Cæsars do to the character of the Imperial city itself. At the same time there arose in our own country that pleiad of conscientious, accurate, and indefatigable Irish scholars, the Petries and O'Donovans and O'Currys—who deciphered and unearthed and made light in the dark places, confounded the scoffers, and convinced every scientific thinker in Europe for all time that the rotting manuscripts to which Irish enthusiasm had clung throughout centuries of unexampled horror were not the mere abracadabra of the fanatical worshippers of a barbarous *patois*, but were the authentic title-deeds of a social system, a history and a literature more venerable and more fascinating than any European race, except the Romans and the Greeks, can produce.

The Gaelic enthusiasts were vindicated. But the Gaelic tongue, while it is honoured in the schools, has been dying on the hills. The masters of many languages take off their hats to it, but to the Irish youth, whom it has suckled, whose mental atmosphere, so to say, it has provided, whose blood pulses with its inspirations, it is still a stranger—an uncouth, ill-clad, poor relation at the door. I do not preach any sudden or violent diversion of our national energies from the channels in which they are now directed, for a National Parliament is the life-giver without which no national interest can flourish, and in whose heat all fair and seemly accessories of national life are sure to blossom forth again. I am fully persuaded that any general Gaelic revival will not come as a mere matter of national penance for past forgetfulness, much less on the terms of penalising the use of that agglomeration of languages which is called the English. It will have to be proven that the language of our fathers is a pleasure and a luxury to the Celtic tongue and brain, even as the hurling and the hunting sports of our fathers have been proven to be an exhilaration to Celtic brawn and muscle. Poor human nature will have to be convinced that a knowledge of the Irish language, in place of being a thing to blush for and disown, a mark of inferiority to be concealed like the faint dark circle around the finger-nails of the octoroon, ought to be the first object of an Irish Nationalist's young ambition, a new sense, a delicious exercise of the faculties, the key that unlocks to him the old palaces, and the old hunting-grounds of his dreams, the music which comes ringing down the ages from the lips of the saints who chanted in the old abbeys, of the warriors whose lusty shouts rang over the old battlefields, and of the lovers who whispered by the haunted Irish springs. Approached thus with the loving ardour of a nation's second youth, the tongue of Tara and Kinkora may realise the fond prophecy that ' the Gaelic will be in high repute yet among the music-loving hosts of Eirinn,' and the men who clung to it when it was persecuted, who believed in it when it was scorned, who in the watches of the night hoped on beside what seemed to be its bed of death, may yet taste the reward of knowing that they have preserved unto the happier coming time a language which will be the well-spring of a racier national poetry, national music, national painting, and of that richer spiritual life of simplicity, of equality, of good-fellowship, of striving after the higher and holier ideals, with which the Celtic race alone seems to have the promise of brightening the future of a disenchanted world.

ARE THE IRISH EVICTED TENANTS KNAVES ? [1]

How do the landlords propose to account for their rage
over the determination to submit the case of the Irish
evicted tenants to public investigation ? They, and
Mr. Balfour as their protagonist, have made English platforms ring for years past with denunciations of the Irish
agrarian combinations. Who has not listened to Tory
orators red to the roots of their hair with indignation
against the dishonesty, immorality, and bloodguiltiness of
the Plan of Campaign ? How many Primrose Dames are
there who do not figure it vaguely to themselves as a conspiracy of thriving tenants and criminal agitators, begun
with the intention of cheating good landlords of their
moderate rents, and carried on by means of cattle hough-
ing and shooting in the legs, until it was at last grappled
with and put down by Mr. Balfour of glorious and immortal memory ? Why does the Tory heart sink at the
proposal to subject the doings of Mr. Balfour and of his
wicked enemies to the cold light of an official Commission ?
A Tory Ministry forced the Parnell Commission on the
House of Commons by the gag, *dum* Pigott *erat*. Ten
years of Irish history was not considered too wide a
space for three Unionist judges to roam over in the quest
for matter discreditable to the Irish cause. It may be

[1] Published in the *New Review* for October, 1892.

presumed that Mr. Morley will not follow the example
set by the late Mr. W. H. Smith, and appoint an Evicted
Tenants' Commission of three Nationalist members of
Parliament.   The combinations to be inquired into are
few and definite. Mr. Balfour's view of them is on record.
They were born of dishonesty, conducted by crime, and
disposed of once for all by Coercion. Here are questions
of facts easily ascertainable, one way or the other. What
better salve could be applied to Mr. Balfour's wounded
feelings than an official exposure of the wickedness of the
thousands of persons he was obliged to evict and cast into
prison, and an imperishable record of the triumphant
results which attended his heroic proceedings ? Nevertheless, the proposed Commission does not excite the same
enthusiasm in Tory breasts as the *Times*' Commission. It
is a notable fact that the merits or demerits of any combination under the Plan of Campaign have never been,
to this hour, investigated in a court of justice. In the
Coercion Courts any reference to the crushing character of
the rents, or to the landlords' unreasonableness, was invariably ruled to be irrelevant. When, in the case of the
Mitchelstown estate, I proposed to show that the evictions
I denounced were fixed for a few days before the Royal
Assent to the Land Act of 1887, and that my remarks had
the effect of protecting the tenants from an attempt to
defraud them of the benefits of that Act, I was informed
by my Removable judges that that had nothing to do with
the case. In the case of each and every agrarian combination formed since 1886, the tenants have courted
arbitration and, failing that, public investigation. They
have done so, I hope to be able to show, for the same
reason for which the landlords and coercionists have as
steadily set their faces against either arbitration or investi-

gation—namely, because the facts prove that the evicted
tenants have been turned out of their homes, not through
any dishonesty or criminality of their own, but through the
astounding folly of Mr. Balfour, who deliberately shut
them out from the Land Act of 1887, and marked them
down as victims of landlord vengeance and coercionist
braggadocio.   Furthermore, investigation will prove that
the attempt (in Mr. Smith-Barry's notorious phrase) to
'make an example' of the evicted tenants ignominiously
failed ; that, after bombarding those couple of dozen bodies
of Irish peasants with every conceivable weapon of Coercion
for five years, Mr. Balfour left every one of the little
peasant combinations unbroken just where he found them ;
and that, consequently, the reputation of a successful
coercionist, wherewith he managed to exalt himself and
ruin his party, is a matter that will bear close public
inquiry no better than the late Mr. Pigott's forged letters.

The initial fact to be borne in mind is that, at the
passing of the Land Act of 1887, not more than fifty of
the Campaign tenants had been evicted—my belief is not
above a dozen.   Seventeen hundred families who have
been since dispossessed were still safe by their firesides.
The thousands of Coercion prosecutions, the police fusillades,
prison scenes, and burnings of evicted cabins with paraffin
oil, which disgraced Ireland for five years and lost the
General Election for the Tories, had not yet taken place.
A statesman of good sense might have then and there
closed the Plan of Campaign chapter in peace, if he had
recognised that the Campaign combinations were simply
a rough-spun remedy for an admitted evil.   He had only
to insert in the Act of 1887 a clause entitling the
Campaigners to the benefits of the Act their own exertions
had secured for their brother tenants.   For example, Lord

Lansdowne's judicial tenants at Luggacurran in 1886 claimed a reduction of 15 per cent. Lord Lansdowne, like Lord Salisbury, swore by all his gods that autumn that he would not abate judicial rents by one farthing. The Land Act of the following year declared that the judicial rents must be abated nevertheless, and 13 per cent. was the reduction which the law compulsorily made in that very Luggacurran division. The Act of Parliament, therefore, established that the tenants were right and Lord Lansdowne wrong. Had the tenants been admitted honestly to their 13 per cent. the struggle in Luggacurran would have been over five years ago. When the Act passed, however, the tenants were under notice of eviction. The whole estate has since been cleared of its population, and Lord Lansdowne is at present invoking the aid of the House of Lords to pull down the wooden huts in which his homeless tenantry have found shelter. It was so all over the country. To proscribe the Campaign tenants as *hostes humani generis*, to hunt them down, wild-game fashion, by way of warning to the Irish tenantry of the unforgivable sin of combination and of Mr. Balfour's prowess as a coercionist, became the settled policy of Mr. Balfour and his landlord confederates. 'If I were an Irish landlord I should rather beg my bread than yield to the Plan of Campaign,' said Mr. Balfour in the House of Commons. Mr. Smith-Barry organised a syndicate of wealthy Englishmen to 'make an example' of the Ponsonby tenantry. The Irish people, for their part, knew that the Campaign tenants, if they were pedantically speaking wrong, were in truth and substance right. They determined they would not tamely submit to see these men exterminated. There followed five years of police terrorism, of cruel evictions, of all those

G

incidents which have landed the Tory party on the left of
the Speaker's chair. The tenants won in many cases, the
landlords won in none; and now that the struggle has
cost the landlords and the British taxpayers probably five
hundred times the amount of the original rent disputes, it
is found that Mr. Balfour's squalid exploits were a gross
and cruel blunder from beginning to end, and his successor
is asked to do the thing which, if it had been done in 1887,
would have saved the Tory Administration five years of
disreputable misconduct and inevitable defeat—namely, to
cease persecuting those seventeen hundred homeless peasant
families, and cast about for some sensible means of re-
admitting them to the little cabins from which they were
driven in the interests of Mr. Smith-Barry's claim to a
peerage and of Mr. Balfour's fame in the Habitations of
the Primrose League.

In the salad days of the late Government the dishonesty
of the Campaign tenants and the shining virtues of their
landlords were insisted upon in tones of thunder. ' Organised embezzlement ' was Lord Salisbury's characterisa-
tion of the tenants' ethics. I wonder how many of the
Campaigned landlords will attempt to take up that brave
position before a Commission empowered to inquire into
facts and figures? The tenants struggled against rack-
rents that were crushing them into the earth. They
sought reductions smaller than the Land Courts would
have awarded them, if they had not been of set purpose
excluded from legal relief. The so-called ' rich ' tenants,
whose dishonesty was the special horror of pure-souled
rack-renters, because they made common cause with their
poorer and more helpless brethren, were simply men not
yet reduced to actual beggary, but whose rents were even
more iniquitous than those of their pauper neighbours, and

who have had to face the larger share of the suffering and self-sacrifice of the common struggle. It is safe to predict that at this time of day no serious attempt will be made to deny that the evicted tenants are the victims of heartless landlord embezzlement—the prey of a system of dishonesty which Lord Salisbury's own Government was coerced into restraining by Act of Parliament. The Clanricarde and Ponsonby estates include one-fourth of the total number of evicted Campaigners. No human being has yet been found to say an apologetic word for Lord Clanricarde. His own leading counsel could not help designating his clearances as 'the devil's work.' 'Lord Clanricarde,' wrote the *Times* newspaper in reference to the trial of Joyce *v.* Clanricarde, 'has been proved to have behaved throughout the entire transaction with a baseness and a harshness to his agent and his tenantry which are hardly credible.' Hardly credible even by the late Mr. Pigott's paymaster! Nevertheless, this man of hardly credible baseness has been permitted for eight years past to devastate twenty square miles of country; has been supplied with extra police escorts uncounted for his agents and bailiffs, to accompany them in their walks, protect them in their evictions, and sweep through the country with them, moss-trooper-wise, in their nightly raids for cattle; there were one hundred and fifty Coercion prosecutions against his heart-broken tenantry, long terms of imprisonment, one shocking death in prison, a bare escape from prosecution of a present Cabinet Minister for daring to hold a public meeting upon the estate, and at the present moment there is pending an order of the High Courts to raze the wooden huts that are sheltering the heads of the evicted from the mountain blast. Perhaps Lord Salisbury would kindly favour the Commission with his views as to where the organised embezzlement lies here, or as to what strait-waistcoat less elastic than a British Act of Parliament will restrain a man of the mental turn of the Most Noble the Marquis of Clanricarde from keeping half a county plunged in misery ?

The circumstances of the Ponsonby struggle, and of Mr. Smith-Barry's evil apparition on the scene, are not yet so well understood in England. One of the advantages of the Commission of Inquiry will be to publish those circumstances far and wide in a manner that cannot be disposed of by vapourings upon Primrose platforms. There is a congenital eccentricity to be pleaded for Lord Clanricarde. It will be curious to see what better excuse than ambition for an extinct family title Mr. Smith-Barry will be able to offer for his interposition at the very moment of an amicable settlement on the Ponsonby estate —an estate with which he was wholly unconnected, and whose tenantry his own agent declared to be grossly rack-rented. The proofs to that effect can be piled heaven-high. The tenantry, although they toiled like slaves on their wretched plots, were so poor that years before the present struggle they had to be saved from famine by public relief. Through the agency of Sir John Arnott, landlord and tenants had come so near a settlement that, in the words of the landlord's representative, Mr. Brunker, ' I had hoped to effect such modifications in the tenants' offer as would enable me to recommend it as a full and fair one,' when, all of a sudden, Mr. Smith-Barry announced, in a banquet speech, that he had organised a syndicate of opulent aristocrats to take over the estate bodily from the landlord, and ' make an example of ' the refractory tenantry. He did so. He has evicted two hundred and forty-one out of two hundred and forty-six tenants—practically the entire

population of the estate—and has left ten thousand acres
of land, in Mr. T. W. Russell's phrase, ' waving with
docks and thistles.' And the tenantry upon whom he has
executed this appalling vengeance are the tenantry of
whom Mr. Smith-Barry's own agent, Mr. Horace Townsend, wrote :—

' From what I have seen of the Ponsonby estate I am
sorry to say that I believe the Land Commission, if it ever
goes before it, will reduce the rents on it very heavily.
. . It is quite good enough ground for fighting, the
tenants having required an equal all-round reduction, and
then gone to the Plan of Campaign ; but I consider that
the late agent should have given larger allowances than
20 per cent. on a good deal of the lands, and have had
all re-valued at the commencement of the row, before the
Plan of Campaign was adopted. The existing rates on
light tillage lands, which might have been fair fifteen
or twenty years ago, are far above the present value. A
good deal of land I saw, I was told, was rented at 20s., bu
it will go under the Land Court at 12s., or 13s., and that
is Barter's (the agent of the Landlords' Corporation)
opinion also. I advise Mr. Smith-Barry and the other
members of the syndicate to make public as soon as possible
that they are only fighting the way in which the tenants
want to get the rents down.'

Here we have the inner mind of the landlords revealed
as in a council of war. ' It is quite good enough ground
for fighting,' says this friend of law and order, fighting
being the syndicate's business in life ; but he proceeds to
warn the belligerent landlords that they have no case on
the merits, and that the public must be bamboozled into
the belief that it is not a question of the justice of the
reduction demanded, but of the tenants' unmannerly

deportment in demanding it. A Land Court, blurts out
Mr. Townsend, would be bound to cut down the rents
wholesale, and the agent ought to have offered an adequate
reduction 'at the commencement of the row, *before the
Plan of Campaign was adopted*'; but since the row has
commenced, by the agent's fault, then keep the tenants
out of the Land Courts, evict them to a man, and join
Lord Salisbury in shouting to the British public that it is
all organised embezzlement.   It will be interesting to hear
Mr. Horace Townsend, and his brother agent, Mr. Barter,
explain to the Commission on what principle their syndicate of English capitalists, thus admonished of the
injustice practised upon the tenantry ' at the commencement of the row, *before the Plan of Campaign was adopted*,'
proceeded to cast more than twelve hundred people on the
roadside, and prolong for five years the ' row ' which was
on the point of friendly settlement when they came upon
the scene with their money bags ' to make an example of '
the rent-crushed tenantry for ' the way in which they
wanted to get the rents down.'   Here is disclosed with
brutal candour the landlord conspiracy which Mr. Balfour
spent five years of Coercion in forwarding—and spent in
vain.

Here is also the origin of the Nemesis that overtook
Mr. Smith-Barry on his own estate in Tipperary.   The
Tipperary tenantry knew, on Mr. Smith-Barry's own
agent's authority, that the eviction of the Ponsonby
tenantry was a crime of the blackest dye.   They had precisely the same right to surrender their shops and farms
to Mr. Smith-Barry that he had to make examples of
the Ponsonby men.   The difference between them was that
he was appealing to wealth and brutal coercion for the
aggrandisement of his own class, while they were making

an unparalleled sacrifice of their property in order to dissuade their landlord from one of the darkest crimes ever perpetrated in Irish landlord history towards men too poor and broken to defend themselves. The more the Tipperary struggle is tested by keen inquirers, the more quickly the absurd impressions generated in the English mind upon the subject by the misrepresentations of Messrs. Balfour and Smith-Barry will vanish, and the more incontestably it will be proved that the abandonment of Mr. Smith-Barry's town and lands in Tipperary was as heroic a deed of self-sacrifice as ever men performed for their weaker fellow-men. Even by the lower test of success in 'making an example of' the devastator of the Ponsonby estate, the New Tipperary exodus was, until the moment of the disruption of the Irish party, a series of amazing triumphs over the infamous influences employed to quell it. I shall be delighted to meet Mr. Smith-Barry at the witness-chair of the Evicted Tenants' Commission on Tipperary topics.[1]

The evicted tenants' justification ' at the commencement of the row, before the Plan of Campaign was adopted ' may now be taken as conceded ground. Another of the outcries against the Campaign combinations with which Tory platforms once reverberated—namely, their criminal character—has long ago been silenced. I doubt whether any witness before a Commission of Inquiry would deny that the Campaign fight has been the means of saving the country for the past six years from agrarian crime, instead of promoting it. The statistics are irresistible. Five fearful agrarian murders took place on the Clanricarde estate in the years prior to the Plan of Campaign ; not one since. Not a single deed of bloodshed has been perpetrated on

[1] The landlords, as was here anticipated, shirked the investigation on a transparent pretext.

the Ponsonby estate among the fifteen hundred persons
who were left homeless there. The attempt to trace crime
to the Tipperary combination was laughed out of court
even by two Removables of the strong-stomached type
of Messrs. Shannon and Irwin. The lives lost during the
reign of Balfourism in Ireland were all taken by Mr.
Balfour's ministers: three men shot on the square of
Mitchelstown by the police; John Mandeville wilfully
murdered in Tullamore Gaol (according to the finding of a
coroner's jury); Patrick Larkin, son of a Clanricarde evicted
tenant, done to death in Kilkenny Gaol; Hanlon run
through the body with a bayonet on the Ponsonby estate;
Kavanagh shot dead by an emergency man on the Coolgreany estate; a boy named Heffernan, fourteen years of
age, shot down by the police in the main street of Tipperary; a Tipperary shopkeeper, named McGrath, found
dead in Clonmel Gaol; and so on. The corpses were all
Nationalist; the lethal weapons all official. There is one
unanswerable crime-test in relation to the Plan of Campaign. Of the only 'crimes' the most keen-scented Removables could detect in the Plan of Campaign twenty-
three members of the House of Commons were convicted.
Those convictions were duly read out by the Speaker to the
House, and even the Government that sent the Pigott
forgeries before three judges had not the hardihood to ask
its Tory majority to express a more than Platonic horror
of these three-and-twenty criminals in their midst by
treating them to the vote of expulsion so liberally exercised
against various non-Irish criminals of another stamp
during the late Parliament.

There are those, indeed, who, waiving the question
whether the tenants were not right ' at the commencement
of the row,' and free from criminal reproach during its

continuance, take refuge in the plea that, their farms having now passed into other hands, Parliament cannot be asked to remake history in order to reinstate them. This is a small point, and in the main an unreal one. There are not fifty cases all told in which the evicted tenants have been replaced by genuine agricultural tenants. No evicted farm has been taken on the Clanricarde or Ponsonby or Olphert estates. The only Tipperary evicted tenant whose property has been laid hold of by an incoming tenant is a man whose house was taken as a Post Office by the late Government as a piece of barefaced partisanship and pecuniary encouragement to Mr. Smith-Barry. The Coolgreany, Luggacurran, and Massereene estates are the only ones on which ' planters ' have been even nominally settled, and the Commission will have a delightful field for inquiry as to the bona-fides of most of these stage tenants. Mr. Townsend Trench, who was agent of the Luggacurran estate, went to Ulster after the evictions in search of new tenants with capital and pluck. He related humorously the result : ' I found a good many who had the capital but not the pluck, and a good many who had the pluck but had no capital.' Mr. Townsend Trench came away and was dismissed from the agency. But another was found who from the ends of the earth collected a band of ' landless resolutes '; to these Dugald Dalgetty levies the farms of the evicted tenants have actually been sold under the Ashbourne Act at the risk of the British taxpayer, contrary to the public protest of the late Land Commissioner MacCarthy ; and the British taxpayer will have some interesting reading as to the uses made of British gold in subsidising landlord misconduct in Luggacurran. It is possible that here and there some honorarium in hard cash may be the easiest way of disposing of any of these ' planters ' who are not merely

emergency men in receipt of regular wages for personating
agriculturists of stern Loyalist principles. The amount of
viaticum necessary to buy off a couple of dozen public
disturbers of that sort is the most twopenny-halfpenny of
considerations in the problem of pacifying a country, in
which the equitable reinstatement of the evicted tenants
is the first and last of axioms.

Driven from all their other old victorious war-cries
against the tenants' combinations—the fault ' at the commencement of the row, before the Plan of Campaign was
adopted ' fixed on their own shoulders out of the mouths of
their own prophets ; the guilt of continuing the row and
of the blood shed in its progress pertaining wholly to
themselves and to the tenants not at all—it seems as if the
landlord syndicate and their advocates in the Press are now
about to concentrate themselves, as upon a last redoubt,
on the position that, be the tenants right or wrong, criminal
or stainless, at all events the Plan of Campaign was insti-
tuted for political purposes, and was therefore a work of
the devil with which there must be no compromise. The
Times takes this view with much self-complacency. It
thinks it has disposed of the whole case for the reinstatement of the evicted tenants when it cites Mr. John Redmond's statement that the Plan of Campaign was a political
weapon. Shocking! exclaims the promulgator of ' Parnellism and Crime '—how can you plead for mercy to
evicted tenants after an admission like that ? But the
Times' reasoning now is precisely the line suggested by
Mr. Horace Townsend to the landlord syndicate as their
cue for gulling the British public. You have no case on
the merits : ' make public as soon as possible that you
are only fighting the way in which the tenants want
to get the rents down.' The grotesque thing is that,

in accusing us of fighting the tenants' battle for political purposes, the *Times* does not see that its whole aim now, and the whole aim of the landlord syndicate and of Mr. Balfour's repressive policy for the past five years, is, and has been, for the mere sake of having ' good enough ground for fighting' their own political and class battles, to ' make an example of' tenants whom their own agent warns them were cruelly wronged ' at the commencement of the row, before the Plan of Campaign was adopted.' Assume for a moment that the worst that can be said against us is true—that our one thought was how to embarrass Mr. Balfour, and that Mr. Balfour's and the landlords' one thought was how to save the State—if the evicted tenants are the ' victims' and ' dupes' of political agitators, that surely is an additional reason for rescuing the victims, rather than for ' making an example of them.' Once concede that the tenants' claims were honest to begin with, and that any charge of crime against them is as gross a libel as the charge of dishonesty : was there ever a more savage policy propounded than that these poor peasants must be hunted to the workhouse or to agrarian crime in order to discredit half a dozen politicians whose dupes and victims the *Times* declares the evicted tenants to have been ? That is precisely the theory on which Mr. Balfour and the landlords have been fighting since 1887, to their own ruin and the disturbance of the country. Have they not had enough of the experiment ? or is the country to be delivered over permanently to turmoil which one sensible clause in the Act of 1887 could have put an end to—delivered over, not for the purpose of punishing dishonest or criminal tenants, but of ' finding good fighting ground' against a handful of politicians whose innocent victims the suffering tenants are proclaimed to be ?

Needless to say, the *Times'* charge that the Plan of Campaign was a mere heartless politician's stratagem is a falsehood as stupid and malicious as certain famous Facsimile Letters.   There is nothing I more heartily hope for than that the history of the Plan of Campaign may be categorically investigated in a manner as decisive as the Facsimile Letters.   The charges of dishonesty and blood-guiltiness against it are already given over by all except the most ignorant Tory *claqueurs*.   The charge that it was not organised under the pressure of a terrific agrarian necessity will be still more signally confuted by the plainest facts.   Nothing will be easier than to prove : —

1. That, if Mr. Redmond knows what he means at all by joining the *Times* in stating that the Plan of Campaign was founded for political purposes, Mr. Redmond had no more to do with the founding of the Plan of Campaign and no more knowledge of the circumstances under which it was founded than the editor of the *Times* had.   Mr. Redmond was not even a member of the Organising Committee of the National League, at one of whose meetings the Plan was first resolved upon.   The first time he assumed a leading position was as the leader of the movement for founding New Tipperary, which was a wholly different matter, three years after.

2. That the Plan was devised during the appalling agricultural crisis of the winter of 1886, in consequence of evidence pouring in upon us that the tenantry on various western estates, rendered desperate by their difficulties, and not knowing whither to turn after the rejection of Mr. Parnell's Bill, were on the point of commencing something like a small Sicilian Vespers ; and that its effect was, beyond all doubt, to stop the recrudescence of agrarian crime, as well as to secure to the Irish tenantry

all that—and more than—Mr. Parnell had thought there
was any use in proposing to the House of Commons to
grant.

3. That the Tory Government had themselves recognised the reality of the crisis by appointing General
Redvers Buller an extra-legal dictator for the county of
Kerry, with a roving commission to beat unreasonable
landlords to their knees, and that the Plan of Campaign
was designed to exercise in the other distressed counties
the same indispensable ' vigour beyond the law ' which
General Buller exercised in the county of Kerry alone,
and which the Tory majority had declined to exercise in a
Parliamentary method.

4. That the Tory Government gave a still more
striking recognition of the necessity for the Plan of Campaign and of the success of its teachings by passing, within
six months after its promulgation, a stronger Land Act
than they had rejected with scorn three months before the
Plan was hit upon—a Land Act which is, to all intents
and purposes, a permanent embodiment of the Plan of
Campaign in the pages of the British statute-book.

5. That up to the time of the passing of that Act
there had been substantially no evictions, no prosecutions,
no bloodshed, and no harm done; that we again and
again offered to abandon the Plan of Campaign if the
Campaign tenants were guaranteed the honest benefits of
that Act, which they themselves had won ; and that a
sensible arrears clause tacked on to the Act would have
averted all the evictions, prosecutions, and barbarities
which followed.

6. That then, and ever since, Mr. Balfour's attitude
was summed up in his exhortation to the landlords to ' beg
their bread rather than yield to the Plan of Campaign,'

and the landlords' attitude was summed up in Mr. Smith-Barry's vow to 'make an example of' the Ponsonby tenantry; that, in pursuance of this policy, Mr. Balfour with his coercion machinery, and Mr. Smith-Barry with his syndicate of English capitalists, combined and confederated to 'find a good fighting ground' for proving Mr. Balfour's prowess as a Coercionist, and avenging upon the tenants their crime of successful combination : that their object, brutally avowed, was to shut the portals of the law against the Campaigners, and not to conciliate, but to crush, them ; and that it was in pursuit of this cruel, unstatesmanlike, and disastrous ambition that 1,700 families were evicted, 5,000 persons hauled before Removable Magistrates, and a diabolical police tyranny set in motion.

Finally, that the 'victims' and 'dupes' of the Plan of Campaign are 100,000 leaseholders with twenty to thirty per cent. knocked off their rents, and 150,000 other judicial leaseholders entitled to three years' swingeing abatements; that its other dire results for the Irish people are the suppression of landgrabbing, and a progress of public opinion which makes even Ulster landlord candidates echo a cry for compulsory land purchase; that the most real and illustrious of our 'victims' is Mr. Balfour, cast down from his high place by a movement of public disgust at his five years of vicious and abortive Coercion ; that on ninety-five out of the 110 Plan of Campaign estates the landlords have elected to make a sensible settlement instead of taking Mr. Balfour's advice to beg their bread ; and that, as to the couple of dozen remaining estates on which the Coercionists and Eviction Syndicates have magnanimously concentrated all their forces for years to 'make an example,' the evicted tenantry, if they have endured much suffering of late, owing to the unhappy strife in the National ranks, have at least been saved from hunger up to this hour, have lived to see their merciless evictors ' made an example of ' at the late General Election, and to see a Government installed in power whose mandate it is to respect Irish opinion in Irish affairs, and who must be well aware that the most passionate anxiety of the Irish heart is to see justice rendered to the 1,700 village heroes whom the Balfours and Smith-Barrys conspired in vain to exterminate.

Mr. Morley has only to drag out the facts and fear not.

MR. MORLEY'S TASK IN IRELAND

MR. MORLEY came to Ireland with the powers of a Cromwell; but he is a Cromwell with a Royalist army. Without his majority at Newcastle at his back, he would have had every major official, and most of the minor officials, around him directing operations upon the calculation that he would be overthrown in six months. The shout of ' Fair Play ! ' from the Newcastle democracy has rendered them cautious and complaisant; but they regard Mr. Morley's apparition at the Castle with the same feeling with which ancient retainers would regard Cromwell's top-boots in a Cavalier drawing-room. They simply keep their maledictions under their breath. Why not purge the public service, then, of such servants? Is not the work of ' clearing out the Castle ' the very job Mr. Morley has come to perform? There was just one sound Home Rule official whom the Tories found at the Castle. Their Chief Secretary's first task was to transport him to the Colonies. Why not begin by sending Sir West Ridgway back to Afghanistan, and by putting some man in his place who does not believe the policy of his chief to mean treason and red ruin? But that is just where the difficulty comes in. It is easy for a Tory Chief Secretary to find Sir West Ridgways by the score; but where is Mr.

---

¹ Published in the *Fortnightly Review*, November 1892.

Morley to look for his Sir Robert Hamiltons? The Irish
Tories are incorrigible. The old Presbyterian Liberals of
the North, who are longing for place; who were all but
as complete pariahs as the Nationalists; who, by-and-by,
when the Home Rule Bill is passed, will make invaluable
administrators, remain, and will remain, hostile to Home
Rule so long as it is not quite certain to be carried. Mr.
Morley cannot depend upon the minority to help him with
good candidates. Still less can he look to the Nationalist
majority. There would be no difficulty in picking out
Nationalists competent to administer the Castle depart-
ments as uprightly and well as they have upon the whole
administered the affairs of the City corporations and
Poor-law boards. But a Nationalist will no more enter
Dublin Castle until an Irish Government possesses the keys
than he will go by choice to reside in a cholera hospital.
Even with a Home Rule Chief Secretary at the helm, the
place is in quarantine. The Irish public have the same
sort of sympathy for Mr. Morley as for a gallant surgeon
who embarks in a plague-stricken hulk all alone. The
perversity of Nationalists in crying out against existing
Castle officials, and declining to supply better ones, is the
theme of considerable and amusingly contradictory remark.
Our Redmondite friends, whenever they are particularly
hard up for any intelligible charge against us, affect to talk
of the Irish party as place-hunters; while Mr. Stead
inveighs in strong terms against Mr. Sexton for declining to
be Chief Secretary, and suspects there is something sinister
in the self-denying ordinance observed by the Irish party.
The Redmondites, of course, only use the term 'place-
hunters' because it is less ridiculous than 'seceders,' as
applied to a party of seventy-one by a party of nine.
They are quite well aware that the members of the Irish

H

party have no notion of accepting office under any English Government of Ireland. Outsiders have more difficulty in understanding why Nationalists should not either take up the official burden themselves or cease prating against officialdom. I am not sure there would be much use in trying to explain our position in this respect. It is one of those *cosas de Irlande* which are as evident to us as the greenness of our fields, but which are nevertheless puzzling to our best friends across the Channel, and which are, indeed, themselves unanswerable arguments for Home Rule. Suffice it to say that the Nationalist determination to steer clear of office-seeking does not cover any deep plot against the integrity of the Empire.

The fact stands, however, that Mr. Morley has nothing better than criticism of his officials to expect from the Nationalists and nothing better to expect from most of those officials than the sort of complaisance associated with regard for one's bread and butter. He has also the disadvantage of his good qualities. Mr. Balfour had impressed every official, from the highest to the lowest, with the conviction that, no matter how he sinned from over-zeal, he had only to sin strongly to be promoted by leaps and bounds during Mr. Balfour's tenure of office, and provided with a luxurious place of retreat on any change of Government. The history of Mr. Cecil Roche's progress from a Liberal-Unionist lectureship to a Fishery Inspectorship can be read by the meanest official understanding. Your Irish Removable believes Mr. Morley to be a philosopher, and therefore a fool, who will concern himself more about being scrupulously just to his enemies than about promoting his friends. He showed the teeth of a lion at Newcastle, and they have no notion of testing the sharpness of those teeth by any open revolt; on the contrary,

they all take care to feed the noble animal industriously
with those cates of dispassionate attention to business
which they believe will best impress a strong lover of even
justice ; but they have the comfortable feeling that the lion
is barred safely into an official cage, of which all the keys
are in the pockets of sound Unionists.   Mr. Morley's con-
tingent in the Irish Privy Council is as small as in the
House of Lords.   It must have taken some whipping up
to get together a quorum of three to sign the proclamation
suspending the Coercion Act.   Let him suggest a new
departure to the Local Government Board, to the Board of
Public Works, to the General Prisons Board—he will find
himself in a minority of one.   Does he aim at creating
popular confidence in the Land Commission Court—Mr.
Wrench and friends are there to do him battle, vizors
down, placed beyond the criticism of Parliament, by the
care of Mr. Balfour, upon the everlasting eminence of the
Civil List.   Any sub-commissioners who had the misfortune
to inspire public confidence have been ruthlessly sent to
the rightabout.   Has he any feeling that the Congested
Districts Board is fooling with its million and a half of
Irish money, and ought to do something practical to help
the congested population to the sheep-farms vacant round
about them ?   The Congested Districts Board retort that
Mr. Balfour has secured them a twenty years' tenure of
office by Act of Parliament, and in a civil manner give the
Home Rule Chief Secretary what the French call a foot
of nose. Let him require a Removable magistrate or a police
officer in some critical hour and spot—he has to summon
a few dozen hostile officials before him, and by some rapid
process of anthropometry pick out the man who is least
likely to facilitate a riot, or who was least implicated in
the transactions of the old ' don't-hesitate-to-shoot ' days.

As likely as not, the man of his choice may, nevertheless, be one against whom a coroner's verdict of wilful murder stands uninvestigated. Where is the remedy? There are six or eight great officials—the Under-Secretary, the Assistant Under-Secretary, the Inspector-General of Constabulary, and the Divisional Commissioners especially —who are the Chief Secretary's eyes and arms. Unless he can discover half a dozen real auxiliaries for these great posts, it is difficult to see how he can direct the course of events in Ireland any better than an armless man could drive a four-in-hand. Yet it is easy to imagine Mr. Morley in the sombre gloom of Dublin Castle cudgelling his brain for the names of even half a dozen.

This might well be an insuperable difficulty, were it not that the difficulty is understood by the Irish people. Mr. Morley has not come to show that an Englishman can govern Ireland satisfactorily. He is gaining bitter experience in his own person that, with the best will in the world, the thing is impossible. He is simply administering in an interregnum. The Irish people are shrewd enough to see that they must be content with an honest man's best efforts, without demanding miracles, if the interregnum is not to end by re-establishing the Castle instead of clearing it out. A considerable section of the officials, too, are shrewd enough to understand that a philosopher with the grit of Newcastle in him may be more than a match for the tricks of a provincial circumlòcution office, and they will shape their conduct accordingly.

Moreover, the crass folly of the landlords in attempting to provide a lively winter for Mr. Morley has had an excellent effect in teaching the Irish people to make a liberal allowance for his difficulties. The landlords were, to use an American phrase, too previous. They had a famous opportunity. Mr. Morley's first winter in Ireland is unluckily the worst season of the decade. The Hon. Charles Nugent, when he remarked, after the great fair of Ballinasloe, ' There is no use in publishing our misfortunes ; there is almost no price for cattle,' spoke the universal language of cabin and hall ; and to the disaster of cattle selling at cost price there is added the ruin wrought by a harvest-month of daily rains and floods. It took Mr. Balfour more than a million of Imperial money two years ago to cure a distress not one-fourth so extended. The landlords had only to wait, and there would have been trouble enough for the Government in the course of nature. But they had held back so long to oblige Mr. Balfour, that they could not resist the temptation to rush into the fray with their eviction notices, and help to make the Home Rule Government of Ireland a hell upon earth. The Committee of the Landlords' Convention assure us that the statement ' that the Irish landlords have resolved on instituting ejectment proceedings to embarrass the present Government, which they desisted from enforcing during the régime of the late Government,' is utterly untrue. But the accusation was not that they met to pass a formal resolution declaring war on Mr. Morley ; it was that they commenced the war and are in the thick of it. In the paper which contains the diplomatic note from the Landlords' Convention appears also the following : ' Mr. Arthur Langford, landlord of the Rowles property, served eviction-made-easy notices on nine of his tenantry some years ago. He did not issue summonses or seek to recover possession. He has now, however, served summonses for possession on the nine tenants whom he had converted into care-takers.'

Why did not Mr. Langford summon the Crowbar Brigade before the General Election ? The proofs are as

thick as blackberries that the legal proceedings which the
landlords pretermitted so long as the fate of the Coercion
Government was in doubt are being rigorously threatened
now when the tenants have a tenfold claim to consideration.
If the evictions which were proceeding merrily last month
have been to some extent checked, it is simply because
landlord zeal has overreached itself, and has both put the
tenantry upon their guard against temptations to disturbance, and startled the British public with a discovery of
the true character of Mr. Balfour's eviction policy.   Mr.
Balfour had managed to soothe the British elector into the
belief that actual evictions were decreasing to vanishing-
point.   We warned all concerned in vain that eviction-
notices under the seventh clause of the Act of 1887 were
accumulating at the rate of five thousand a year, and that
it would depend upon the landlords' convenience at what
date all the five thousands might be, without further
ceremony, cast upon the roadside.   The British elector
now realises to his horror that the result of Mr. Balfour's
silent system is, that there are at least twenty thousand, and
probably thirty thousand, Irish farmers who are no longer
tenants, but only caretakers, and who, upon a magistrate's
order, might be left homeless and landless at seven days'
notice.

The landlord zealots who brought us face to face with
such a contingency have unconsciously helped to keep the
public peace.   The average Briton is no more in the
humour to stand thousands of eviction scenes than the
average Irishman wants to make the Home Rule Government of Ireland a turbulent one.   Accordingly there have
been symptoms of a more moderate spirit among the diplomatic section of the landlords.   The nobleman who owns
the country for many miles around where I write—who

draws 20,000*l.* a year out of a specially distressful region, and never lays his eyes upon his estate—last month served rent-processes broadcast. I am told he has just intimated to the tenants that he will not press for the rent until Christmas *if they will pay at once the costs of the legal proceedings taken against them.* What an epitome of Irish landlord wisdom ! A demand is made which it is now admitted it was unwise to make, and the tenants who cannot pay rent are asked to pay law costs for the landlord's blunder. But it is an eloquent hint that landlords of the less needy type have come to see that any attempt to carry things with too high a hand in Ireland this winter might prove even more embarrassing for the landlords' cause than for Mr. Morley. It is possible, therefore, that the very difficulties and the appalling dangers, both to landlords and tenants, of the situation in Ireland this winter may be the best allies of a Government whose business is peace.

Then, one of the advantages of the Evicted Tenants' Commission is that it to a great extent removes the agrarian conflict from the scenes of battering-ram operations and moonlight outrages to the judicial atmosphere of a High Court of Appeal. The tenantry's feelings upon the subject may be summed up thus : If the landlords are wise enough to show a conciliatory spirit, well and good ; if they shirk investigation, they are broken ; if they challenge it, they will be broken all the worse. The landlords, for their part, are in a state of miserable irresolution between the desire to run away from the Commission and the terror of public opinion if they do. They now demand that its sittings shall be secret, and that they shall have liberty to obstruct it at will. They have been more or less shamed out of the attitude of defiant high-and-mightiness taken up for them by the *Times* in relation to Sir James Mathew's

Commission. They shrink from boycotting it, as upon one
pretext or another they will by-and-by shrink from facing
it, having the deadly feeling at their hearts that investigation has invariably proved the Irish landlords to be in the
wrong. While Sir James Mathew's eye is upon them,
those who are only meditating eviction will possibly be cir-
cumspect. Those who may be inclined to reject summarily
all applications for reductions of rent this ruinous winter,
will remember that the result of similar action in 1886 was
that the Tory Government next session suspended the
judicial rents for three years. They will hesitate before
driving a Liberal Government to do likewise.

The difficulty of getting through the winter without an
explosion, in face of hostile landlords, sullen officials, and
a population struggling for bare life against an agricultural
crisis which dismays the stoutest hearts, is, after all, only
the initial difficulty. ' If it is so hard to bind the country
to the peace for three months,' cry the croakers, ' how is your
majority of thirty-eight going to frame in a few months
a permanent Constitution for an island where you have
not merely a Belfast minority bombarding you from one
extreme, but a Dublin minority opening fire from the opposite extreme ? ' The task is a formidable task. Nothing short of genius and a noble enthusiasm for peace
between the two islands will be equal to it. To the men
whose policy of ascendency has had a trial of centuries, and
produced nothing better than ages of civil war suppressed
or overt, may be conceded the proud satisfaction of knowing
that the undoing of their work is no child's-play, and that
the Government which has to pass a Home Rule Bill has a
harder road to travel than a Government which had only
to pass a Coercion Bill. It is because the task is heroically
hard that it has become necessary to confront it. To

Englishmen whose opinions about Ireland are still in a
state of fluidity, the wars of the Shamrock and Ivy between
two bodies of Irish Nationalists must be a grievous
stumbling-block.   It is sometimes forgotten that Irish
Nationalists have only fallen out at all because a majority
of seven-eighths of them were willing to sacrifice even Mr.
Parnell's leadership rather than follow him in tearing
up the compact of peace between the two democracies.
Englishmen would do well to bear in mind also that the
only news their papers print from Ireland is sensational
and, generally, mischief-making news.   For ten years all
they read of the Land League revolution was that a voice
cried ' Shoot them ! ' in the course of a public meeting, or
that a cow was mutilated by some Hibernian Jack-the
Ripper.   The readers of the *Times* are at present entertained
with verbatim reports of every insensate word said by
every insignificant Dissentient in the country ; the more
insensate the word, and the more insignificant the man,
the more liberally the *Times*' space is lavished for their
fame.   How is the busy British reader to bethink him that
all this is a ridiculous travesty of the public opinion of a
country in twenty-five out of whose thirty-two counties Red-
mondism has no more effective following than Theosophy
has in the British shires ?   The great counties of Wexford,
Cork, and Tipperary—the first the focus of the Insurrection of '98, and the two others the nurseries and strongholds
of the Fenian movement—are so completely with us that,
in ten out of their thirteen constituencies, no Redmondite
candidate appeared at all, and in the three they fought
they were ridiculously worsted.   The correspondents of the
English papers live in Dublin, and, among vast masses of
the Dublin workmen the feeling that Mr. Parnell was not
so much wrongly displaced as displaced in the wrong

way unquestionably bears all before it for the moment. Capitals are strangely often at opposite poles from their countries in such matters. M. Yves Guyot was almost the only non-Boulangist deputy returned by Paris at the General Election at which France effaced Boulanger. Dublin did not return a Nationalist member until 1885. That was not the fault of the working masses, who were always intensely Nationalist; but the country cannot forbear smiling at the Dublin Town Councillors who have taken to instructing Cork and Tipperary how to deal with Sassenach Lords-Lieutenant in the high heroic way.

In one respect, the most hopeless feature of our domestic quarrel is that it has no substantial cause which can be comprehended and removed, but is an affair of personal feeling. But this also has its advantages. The personal ill-feeling does not extend to Mr. Morley. Bitter things said in the heat of Committee Room No. 15, where the struggle was, in the nature of things, as fierce as one with guns and pistols on a Parisian barricade, are at the bottom of whatever resentment still survives against the victors. Mr. Morley's way of dealing with the last tragic passages of Mr. Parnell's great life was sympathetic, and even tender. He is known to have co-operated actively in the endeavour to save him by reconciling him to the step which his own councillors without exception favoured. A Dublin crowd may be induced to cross Mr. Morley's policy, but will not be easily brought to think evil of him.

The moment our opponents cease to appeal to the feeling of sorrow for Mr. Parnell's fate—which all honest Irish hearts share to the full as ardently as they—and come to state what practical differences of policy they have to show for their separate existence, the unsubstantiality of the Redmondite feud as a factor in practical politics

becomes at once apparent. The English Tory grows
chilly over Mr. John Redmond's Home Rule article in the
' Nineteenth Century,' as the Tory cheers dried up in the
House of Commons while Mr. Redmond insisted that the
Irish Parliament was to be ' a minor Parliament.' The
Home Rule resolution arrived at the day after the anni-
versary demonstration at Mr. Parnell's grave was in
substance one which, I presume, any meeting of English
Home Rulers would accept as a commonplace. The Irish
people are to have the control of an unarmed police, they
are to have the appointment of their own judges and
magistrates, they are to be at liberty to legislate upon the
land question if the Imperial Parliament itself will not
undertake an immediate and final settlement of the
question. There is nothing new in that. It is as old as
Boulogne. The only points contended for by Mr. Parnell,
at Boulogne, were the above. He did not at all make any
point as to the veto a condition of his retirement. He did
not, of course, raise it in his suggestions to Mr. Gladstone
prior to the Bill of 1886. The veto is a question rich in
pedantic controversies and obstructive possibilities, but of
little practical moment to two nations honestly determined
upon reconciliation. The Colonial Secretary's power of
overhauling the affairs of Canadian and Australian colonies
at will is the veto in the most objectionable form it could
well assume ; and yet what Colonial Secretary's office
would be worth a week's purchase if he proceeded to play
Cæsar over the elected representatives of Victoria or the
Dominion ? There is no difference in essence between the
Liberals and the Irish Party, or between the Redmondites
and either. The supremacy of the Imperial Parliament
is the admitted basis of all negotiations. The Imperial
Parliament could not, if it would, divest itself of the power

of altering or recalling an Act of its own giving. Supremacy, yes; meddlesomeness, no. What we are entitled to
have substantially ensured is that, so long as it acts within
the range of its delegated or exempted powers, the Irish
Parliament shall be free from meddlesomeness or malicious
interposition from Westminster by a majority which, for
all we know, might be a majority led by Mr. Balfour.
That is obviously a requirement as necessary to the
comfort of the Imperial Parliament as to the dignity of
the Irish Parliament, and is the first condition of the
successful working of any Home Rule scheme at all. We
do not believe statesmanship will have more difficulty in
devising a sensible plan by which the Imperial and Irish
Parliaments will move harmoniously together, each in its
own circle, than has been found in grouping the forty-four
American States around Washington, or in keeping
twenty parliaments in healthy activity within the British
Empire. If we decline to discuss this or that particular
plan pending the production of the Home Rule Bill, it is
for the same reason for which we declined to join Mr.
Chamberlain in demanding that details should be discussed
clause by clause before the General Election—namely,
because premature and irresponsible discussion of this
kind, while the proposals of the responsible Government
are in preparation, suits the enemies of Home Rule and
does not suit us. The important point is that, in matters
of substance, as apart from form and pedantry, all Home
Rulers are agreed that the Irish Parliament must have the
full and honest management of Irish affairs ; and a vote
against an honest Irish Parliament out of mere temper
would be the extinction of Parnellism as a Parliamentary
force.

At the same time, as one who has laboured all along,

and at some risk, for reconciliation, and who will never be
a party to closing the door against reconciliation, I cannot
avoid seeing that men are growing into power among our
opponents in whose hands Mr. John Redmond and his
friends are only parliamentary chessmen—men whose
watchword is ' No reconciliation ! '—and who propose to
constitute themselves a permanent element of opposition
in Irish political life.   That I regret deeply, for the poison
it spreads in social life, and the young minds it leads astray ;
but adversaries of Home Rule need not too hastily assume
that a fixed division of opinion among Irish Nationalists
constitutes an argument in their favour.   It, on the contrary, disposes of the old rooted suspicion that the Irish
party were a band of conspirators who would be able to
wield an Irish Parliament without let or hindrance as a
weapon for separation.   It would simply add another
minority to the Opposition benches on College Green, and
would in that way constitute an additional guarantee for
the protection of minorities.   The Orange minority and
the Ivy minority would club together in the Irish Parliament, as they clubbed together in Cork last year, when
they swapped a Redmondite mayoralty against an Orange
shrievalty.   For all practical fighting purposes, the Extreme
Right and the Extreme Left are linked together through
the country as effectively as the Tories and Liberal-Union-
ists pull together in Great Britain.   The bogey of bogeys
in Ulster is the fear of priestly dictation.   The fiercest
Ulster bigot will not complain that he has not sufficiently
ardent Southern Catholic allies now—paladins who are
not content with combating undue clerical influence, but
contest the right of an Irish priest even to give ordinary
constitutional expression to opinions which happen to be
the opinions also of five-sixths of the community.   It is to

the last degree painful and dangerous that, at so critical an hour, we should have two minorities to contend against in place of one. But among misgoverned nations absolute unity is not often to be had, even under the pressure of national emergency. There were seven warring factions among the Greek insurgents when the sympathetic British frigates opened fire in Navarino Bay to give them freedom. If the Irish Opposition of the future is to move its votes of censure before there is an Irish Government to be censured, that is simply one of the pains of self-government which Ireland will have to face slightly before her time, and which Ireland alone will have any right to grumble about. The only polemics a democratic country has any right to proscribe are those of the *argumentum baculinum*. So long as the Belfast minority or the Dublin minority are content to observe the ordinary police regulations in their discussions, they have a right to speak, and hoot, and demonstrate to their liking, and to combine their forces together, whether for Cork municipal honours, or for a coalition ministry in the future, and in proportion to the common sense of their programme and the respect for their character will be their success with the electors. All that British Home Rulers have the right to require is that the Irish people shall put forth a demand which is reasonable by a majority which is decisive. This they have done, in the teeth of unparalleled difficulties, by a more convincing verdict than any by which England ever voted Whig or Tory, or the United States supported Abraham Lincoln in the crisis of the slave war. High above the clamour of the two minorities put together stands the solid phalanx of the Irish Nationalist majority, most of them returned by majorities of thousands in South and North, and ready with an unmistakable programme, and an equally unmistakable determination to enforce it against all comers with patience, toleration, and self-control.   That their programme is not one openly or covertly unfriendly to the British people has just been proved by an ordeal as cruel as ever tested the fidelity of Irish Nationalists.   Our opponents' last hope of a future lies in their prediction that belief in British faith will be ill repaid.   Time has only to falsify the prophets of evil, and Mr. Morley will find forces gathering at his back sufficiently intelligent, strong and stable, not merely to aid him in governing Ireland successfully through a troubled winter, but to take up the work from him under a native administration.   He has a difficult task, but an unexampled opportunity.

TOLERATION IN THE FIGHT FOR IRELAND [1]

A PHILOSOPHER once observed that men are apt to have
less charity for those who believe in half of their creed than
for those who deny the whole of it. The observation is
especially true of politics in our day, and is true, to an
aggravated degree, of Irish politics. Political bigotry has
increased in the proportion in which religious intolerance
has diminished; and with far less justification than could
be quoted for the excesses of religious warfare. Religious
truth is a matter of eternal concern, and appeals to a Divine
sanction. Political truth is the most dubious and change-
able of all the sciences. It has sects without number. Its
tenets and boundaries are shifting with every generation.
Nevertheless, men who would call it mediæval bigotry to
persecute their neighbours for differences about points of
theology are sometimes disposed to consider it the first of
public virtues to display intolerance towards those of our
countrymen who differ from us in complicated political
controversies : to attribute to them the motives of knaves,
and to reply to them with words as harsh as paving-stones,
and in extreme cases even with paving-stones without the
words. We have arrived at a stage in Irish affairs at
which it occurred to me some national benefit might be

---

[1] Lecture delivered before the Belfast Young Ireland Society,
Nov. 2, 1892.

derived from a friendly consideration of the causes which have given our Irish political conflicts an undue tinge of bitterness, and of those sacred principles embedded in the Irish cause which have only to receive free play to make for national unity, largeness of view, and generosity of feeling among our fellow-countrymen, whatever may be their blood, or creed, or rank.

In the first place, be it understood that these remarks will not have reference to the Nationalist dissensions of the hour, which still, to some extent, distract three or four counties.   Happily for you here in Belfast, and indeed north of the Ulster border, domestic faction does not trouble your peace.   Even within the limited area in which it is still a worrying and perplexing element, its fortunes have now sunk to a level at which large allowances can be made for misunderstandings, and some rein given to the noblest passion which possesses the victorious soldier— his sympathy for men who have fought and lost.   I would speak of interests less transient, and of wounds going deeper to our vitality as a nation.   We are on the eve of a battle for our existence as a self-governing nation, as dramatic as if the opposing hosts were arrayed in scarlet and in blue upon the field of Waterloo, and of deeper import for the future happiness of these islands than were all the costly military adventures against Napoleon.   What could be more useful at such an hour than to review those common interests, sympathies, and traditions which constitute us a nation as contra-distinguished from a faction ? What better auxiliary than the proof that the passion of Patriotism appeals to influences more elevated than that of mere political partisanship in the Irish nature—that it possesses richly those inspiring and cementing qualities which are capable of knitting together all the inhabitants of this island—Celtic, Dane, or Saxon—in a common kindred, not indeed exempt from the differences of opinion which are the badge of human frailty, but warmed with a common love for a beautiful country, bound together for better for worse by interests which can no more be severed than the tide of centuries can be rolled back, and ready to face the future government of their native land with the magnanimity which can all but remake a sorrowful history, and render a healthy conflict of opinions the salt of public life, and not its poison ?

In the next place, no particular school of Irish politicians can escape their share of responsibility for the acrimony, the apparent remorselessness, of disputes which the mass of Englishmen discuss rather less excitingly than the day's racing news, and which Americans blot out of their memory the morning after a Presidential election. We are all sinners by the temptation to over-zeal. It runs in our blood. It has been implanted in us by our history. Fervid conviction, a quickness of vision which realises our own point of view so intensely that it becomes difficult to imagine any other, the soldier-instinct which once enlisted under a sacred banner will charge with the impetuosity of crusaders and will cling all the more devotedly to a losing side, are all qualities which make bad disputants but charming comrades. In this respect, as in so many others, the virtues and the foibles of battalions in Orange and battalions in Green resemble one another as closely as the pavements of Carrick Hill resemble the pavements of the Shankhill Road. On both sides there is the same heat, the same whole-hearted faith in their own way of thinking ; the same swiftness to carry the argument from words to blows ; and the same chivalrous acknowledgment of opponents' good qualities the moment the clash of the battle is

over. The Irish over-readiness to commence a quarrel, and
the still more Irish eagerness to forget it, are typified in the
story of Grattan, who rushed to the Fifteen Acres to shoot
the Chancellor of the Exchequer, and then watched by his
bedside with the tenderness of a Sister of Charity. They
are illustrated still more vividly by his encounter with his
illustrious fellow-countryman, Henry Flood. Their quarrel
left to the schoolboys of all ages two masterpieces of invec-
tive, and to the Irishmen of all ages the regret that two of
the greatest figures in our history should have marred
their glory by a contest so vulgar in a moment so sublime.
There are few pleasanter things in Grattan's noble story
than to know that only a few days afterwards he was peni-
tentially unsaying his sarcasms of that stormy hour, and
endeavouring to compensate from a good heart for the
exuberance of a rash genius. Two English statesmen in
the same circumstances would probably have whispered
their impressions of one another in smoke-rooms or jotted
them down with a pen of poison in their diaries, instead of
vociferating them in the House of Commons. England
would have suffered less by the backbiting than Ireland
did by the hard-hitting; but, worldly wise interests apart,
it is not certain that human nature is any the greater
sufferer by the open folly than by the secret malice.

But we need not look for the secret of Irish quarrelsomeness in any ingrained bias of the race, when we
have but to investigate any of the feuds which divide
Irishmen to see that these feuds have been specially created
by our English governors for the purpose of keeping Irish
classes and creeds asunder. Irish quarrelsomeness is
English policy. It is not a provision of nature. It is the
invention of cunning conquerors. One of the grotesque
assumptions of the opponents of Home Rule is that the

Irish population is composed of two races who have never melted together, and can never by any possibility melt together. The evidence of history is all the other way. It is true that English policy has invariably aimed at the creation of an English settlement, which was to stand apart from the native population as disdainfully as an English regiment operating in the country of the Hottentots. With that object she endowed her colonists with every privilege that could give them an interest in hectoring the natives. She hemmed them around with every barrier that legislation and religion could build between them and the mere Irish. But the result in all ages has been the breaking down of the barriers, the identification of the colonists with the natives, and the substitution of some fresh English garrison for the purpose of despoiling and hunting down the English garrison which preceded them. If ever there were colonists firmly planted, they were the irresistible knights, each of them in his armour all but as impregnable as a modern ironclad, whom Strongbow left in possession of the land with none but half-naked Celtic clans, emaciated by three centuries of Danish invasions, to dispute it ; yet before two hundred years were over there was scarcely a descendant of Strongbow's knights who was not branded with treason to the English interest. They spoke the Irish tongue. They loved the Irish land, they defied English statutes to seek the hands of Irish wives. The ' degenerate English ' they were called, and they were deprived of their heads for attempting to make themselves at home in Ireland, as a more modern English garrison are about to be deprived of their ascendency for sinning the other way. With the exception of Hugh O'Neil and stainless Hugh O'Donnell, who practically held Ulster as sovereign princes, Queen

Elizabeth's troops had more Fitzgeralds, Butlers, Barrys, Bourkes, and Fitzmaurices of English blood to encounter than Gaelic chiefs. A new English garrison took possession of the lands and privileges of the old one. Religion was erected as a new and impassable boundary of the Pale. Bigotry was to a large extent set up as a protection against identification with the Irish enemy, which was more likely to generate savage ferocity between the two nations than the Statute of Kilkenny's fulminations against Irish dress and Irish sweethearts. But its Protestantism did not preserve the English colony from the whims of its London masters. Still another English garrison which was Royalist was swept aside by a fresh English garrison which was Roundhead ; and the English Parliament was dividing the lands and chattels of Anglo-Saxon Castlehavens, Prestons, and Bellings among its latest Cromwellian favourites. There came other lurches of English opinion from Puritan gravity to Congreve's plays, and from the restoration of one king to the chasing of another; and once more the English garrison in Ireland fared ill on both sides. Walker's death was the subject of a sneer from King William while he was actually crossing the Boyne ; and the most illustrious names in the opposite camp were those of Sarsfield, the Anglo-Irish Protestant, Talbot the Englishman, and Sir Richard Nagle, the Norman. It would seem as if the last precaution that diabolical ingenuity could suggest to dissever the English garrison from Irish sympathies was taken when the Penal Laws were devised for the purpose of giving the colonists a power over the goods, bodies, and souls of the subject Irish more debasing and minute than was claimed by any modern code of slavery. But the unconquerable assimilative force of Irish patriotism was too strong even for the Penal Laws.

The horrid statutes of Anne were not fifty years in force before we had Protestant Lucas repudiating the right of England to subject Ireland to her laws. They were not eighty years in force when we had Protestant Volunteers discharging their cannon in celebration of Irish National Independence; when we had Protestant Wolfe Tone drawing up his declaration of fraternity with his Catholic fellow-countrymen; and when we had the Presbyterians of the North storing up their pikes and guns by tens of thousands to fight for Irish freedom on the field, and making the streets of Belfast ring with the joyous anthem that 'The French were on the sea.'

English policy up to that point had proceeded upon the plain principle of breeding an Irish colony to be the bribed enemies and oppressors of their native fellow-subjects, and superseding every colony that lapsed from that duty by a new colony which ate up the lands and power of its predecessor. Pitt for the first time hit upon the device of utilising the native Catholic millions against the rebellious Protestant and Presbyterian colonies. He could not forgive the Protestants for the Declaration of Independence, nor the Presbyterians for Antrim fight; and, in order to carry the Union, he proceeded to ply the Catholics with the same degrading argument that is pressed upon Protestants at the present moment against Home Rule— namely, that they could not trust their own countrymen not to oppress them; that they must look for emancipation and wisdom and privilege to a stranger Parliament in Westminster. Pitt, of course, betrayed the Catholics, as he had betrayed the Protestants. More Catholic relief was enacted by the Protestant Irish Parliament of 1795 than could be wrung out of the *United Parliament for one generation after the Union. There came a day when

English statesmen began dimly to realise the gigantic
blunder of English policy in Ireland for ages in bribing
the few to oppress, degrade, and revolt the many.   There
began the inevitable process of unloading the few of the
unjustifiable privileges which England for her own
purposes had heaped upon them.   Their religious establishment had to be reduced to equality.   Its ascendency
meant slavery of soul to four-fifths of the population.
Their despotic power of rack-renting had to be shorn away.
Its continuance meant not merely degradation of spirit,
which blighted industry, but physical hunger, which con-
signed hundreds of thousands of people to famine-graves
in every generation.   These were painful surgical operations for a class bred up to pride and sway.   They were
all the more painful that the surgery was slow, and
bungling and indecisive.   As the passions of the hour
evaporate we will more and more come to feel sympathy,
rather than resentment, against a class who have been
stripped of privilege so painful to part with, and whose
fault was almost one of historic necessity.   I have often
thought that a great English statesman at the commencement of this century, if he proposed to reverse the policy
of centuries and reduce the English garrison in Ireland into
citizens in place of tyrants, ought to have treated the
Irish question as England treated the negro slave question
—that is to say, by recognising that the dominion of the
Irish landlord caste was the legacy of a fatal English
policy, and by giving liberal pecuniary compensation to
the class whose domination the national interest compelled
him to dethrone and disendow.

But, whatever clumsy ill-doing may be charged against
England, either in arming her Irish garrison for mischief
or in disarming them with kicks and cuffs as soon as the

mischief is found out, it is certain that the Irish dominant class have contributed most of all to their own destruction, by refusing to identify their cause with that of their own countrymen, and by failing to recognise that the old barbaric policy of loading a minority with power and riches to oppress the majority could never become English policy again. That I take to be the central folly of the Irish landed men—their wild hope that the English masses can ever again be brought to think it to be England's interest that five-sixths of the population should be ground into enemies and serfs and famine-victims in order to keep a well-fattened minority in good humour. They may as well hope to see the Imperial Parliament re-enacting the laws against an Irish glibb or outlawing Irish wives. To their own woe, they have never yet responded to the passionate appeals of generations of Irish patriots to them to trust to their own countrymen, instead of relying upon the hope of poisoning the prejudices of an English faction against the kindly children of the Irish soil. A number of years ago, in a lecture from which much might have been expected, a young Irish nobleman, Lord Monteagle, laid down, I think accurately, the two conditions on which the Irish gentry might even yet enjoy careers of honour and might in their own country. The first condition was that they should cease to be landlords, and the second was that they should cease to act as the English garrison. The conditions are by no means so onerous as they seem; and they are conditions which are, in any case, as inevitable as vote by ballot. Compulsory purchase is emplanked in Lord Frederick Hamilton's programme as firmly as it is in ours. And the man who expects the English democracy ever again to give sovereign power to an English garrison for the purpose of making enemies of the Irish race may live in hopes of seeing rewards published once more for school-masters' or friars' heads. Nevertheless, I have never heard Lord Monteagle's voice raised since to preach his wholesome gospel to his class; and his class, instead of hearkening to the warning, place all their hopes for the future in being able to persuade genteel English audiences that their own fellow-countrymen are a race of knaves and cutthroats, and that the business of an English garrison is to hold them down in bonds of steel. I only desire at this moment to mark that the Irish dominant class have no right to blame their own countrymen for their misfortunes. They must place them to the account of English folly of the past, and of their own folly in the present in imagining that they can revivify in the broad nineteenth century the discarded English policy of the Dark Ages. There is nothing in the nature of things to prevent their being more honoured figures in an Irish Parliament than in an English Primrose Habitation. The choice lies with themselves. They have to opt between the status of Irish citizens and of disbanded English mercenaries. One honest act of identification with their own countrymen, and they will have turned ' old rusted hates into the gold of love.'

If that is true of the class with whom the Irish masses have had to wrestle in long and bloodstained fight for the bare right to live, how immeasurably more artificial and unreal are the barriers which divide the Irish Nationalist majority from the Presbyterian farmer toiling on the hills of Tyrone, or from the Orange Trade-Unionist in Belfast, nursing his dreams of a brighter future for Labour ! The bond of a separate nationality which Tory politicians have constructed, for the past twelve years, between the land-lords and the Protestant farmers of Ulster, between the capitalists and the Orange workmen of Belfast, is an invention so spurious that nobody less ignorant of the affairs of Ireland than that characteristic Ulsterman, Mr. Arnold Forster, would take it seriously. It is easy enough, indeed, to understand why the landlords should be eager to separate the Presbyterian farmers from their Catholic brethren, and why the capitalists of Belfast should prefer to see their stubborn Orange workers listening to Colonel Saunderson denouncing Home Rule, rather than see them, with their labour banners outspread, marching shoulder-to-shoulder with their Catholic brother-workers, as happened not many moons ago, to the consternation of Unionists who are not Trades-Unionists. But we will seek high or low in vain for any reciprocal reason why the Presbyterian democracy in the country, or the Orange democracy in the towns, should foregather with the ruling class in hall and factory as kith and kin, and play their game and draw out their chestnuts from the fire, rather than claim kinship with the majority of their fellow-countrymen, rough-fisted and toil-worn like themselves, who have made it possible for a Presbyterian farmer to live and thrive, and who are in the forefront of the movement for revolutionising the lot of all who toil. The Ulster aristocracy of land and trade claim two bonds of kindred with the non-Catholic masses—the claim of race and the claim of religion. It is only in very recent years the claim has been insisted upon. The cry of a common religion was not heard when the Protestant farmers of County Down were expelled by tens of thousands in the clearances which gave the American Revolution its stout Irish Protestant soldiers. The sacrosanct tie between lord and yeoman was not loudly proclaimed in the days when the Presbyterian hearts of steel swept into Belfast and captured the gaol there. The Ulster Presbyterians were not so richly feasted with offices nor petted on baronial platforms in the days of landlord power, that they need be much impressed with the fear of persecution from the Catholics, who effected Presbyterian as well as Catholic Emancipation, and by whose struggles Presbyterian homesteads have become secure against tyrant blows.

The argument as to race breaks still more ridiculously down. The Irish, who never persecuted a man yet for his religion, are expected to begin with half-a-million of Presbyterian countrymen, who almost within cannon-shot of Antrim shores have millions of Scottish kinsmen and co-religionists beyond the Mull of Cantyre who are all but as eager Home Rulers as those of Cork or Tipperary. The argument that the Ulster Presbyterians can never be whole-souled Irish Nationalists because their ancestors came from Scotland three hundred years ago is not a whit less absurd than would be the argument that the Highlanders must be irreconcilable Irish rebels because their ancestors came out of Ireland a not very much longer time before. But speculation one way or the other is, in truth, ousted by fact, hard, recent, and undeniable. For before our grandfathers' hair was grey, Protestant patriotism and Presbyterian patriotism were as much the commonplaces of everyday life in Ulster as an anti-Home Rule article in the *Belfast Newsletter* is to-day. If Ulster Presbyterian was not penetrated to the core with the passion of Irish freedom, Presbyterian blood must have been shed on the battlefields and the scaffolds of Ulster under an extraordinary delusion, and a grandfather of a certain eminent Unionist judge of our acquaintance must have been hanged by some very singular mistake. There died less than a dozen years ago near Cave Hill an old man who remembered to have seen the streets of Belfast waving with Presbyterian

banners, on which was inscribed, not an ode to Mr. T. W.
Russell, but the revolutionary watchword:

> France is free,
> So may we,
> Let us will it !

These are facts of not very much less recent occurrence
than the arrival of Mr. Arnold Forster in Ulster politics,
and of slightly more authenticity than Mr. Arnold Forster's
anecdotes. To set down as irreclaimable anti-Irish Irishmen a race of Ulstermen who could not search an old
family wardrobe without finding a uniform of the Volunteers, or the thatch without finding the pike of a United
man, or the family gravestone without discovering a grandfather shot or hanged in the patriot cause, is an insult to
a schoolboy's knowledge of Irish history, as well as an outrage upon the memory of as stout a band of warrior patriots
as ever flung the Green Flag to the winds and bade their
Catholic fellow-countrymen muster hand-in-hand with them
under its folds.

The fact is that, while the Irish race is of as distinctive
a type as any of the great divisions of mankind, it is a
type which is evolved from a dozen sources all blending in
the sunheat of Irish nationality as harmoniously as the
rivulets leap from the Irish hillsides in the sparkle of the
all-embracing sun. Certain grand characteristics survive
every mutation, and are reproduced unconquerably, whether
the material added to the crucible be Gaelic, Norman,
Saxon, or Palatine. But it is a race above all things assimilative, from which you could no more abstract the blood
of three hundred years ago than you could distinguish
the Gael from the Firbolg or the Firbolg from the Tuatha
de Danaan of enchantment. If you sought the authentic
doctrine of nationality accepted by all Irish Nationalists of

to day, you would find it, large 'as our holy island and liberal as the mountain breeze, in the principles instilled into the *Nation* newspaper by Thomas Davis. What Irish Nationalist ever proposed to open Thomas Davis's veins to discover whether the orthodox quantity of Gaelic blood flowed to his heart ? Were the question of race-origin a vital one the day that Davis, Duffy, and Dillon came together in the Phœnix Park to found their newspaper, they would instantly have fled apart into three camps ; for the three men were of three bloods—Norman, British, and Gaelic. Were we to enter a National Portrait Gallery under the influence of this bigoted one-stem theory of our far-branching race, we should have to commence by tearing down the likenesses of three-fourths of the men whom the universal Irish heart reveres and loves, and we should have to seek our heroes mostly in ages before portraits began to be painted. We should be doing just as wise and feasible a thing as if the English people were to set about picking out every Englishman whose ancestor had been at the wrong side at the battle of Hastings, and banishing them to Normandy on the ground of incompatibility of race-temperament.

The three great race-elements of our population are knit together by every moral and material tie that could consecrate the partnership of men born under the same sky, and harnessed together for the same work in life. Even by the tie of religion—for all three are penetrated alike with veneration for those Divine revelations and those principles of Christian morality which they believe to be the basis of all human society. By the tie of material interests—for we may defy the most ingenious separatists to draw a line of distinction between the wants, the labours, and the ambitions of the farmer by the banks of the Bann and those of the farmer by the banks of the Lee, or between the future of Labour as pictured on the Limerick Dockers' quay and as pictured in the workshops of the Queen's Island. By the tie of common suffering in a common national cause, too—for there is scarcely an Ulster Protestant towards whose grandfather's Volunteer corps the hearts of the Southern Catholics did not go out, and there is scarcely an Ulster Presbyterian whose grandfather did not hear of the battles of the Wexford Insurrection with eye as bright and blood as throbbing as if he were encamped on the victorious crest of Oulart Hill. It is idle to suppose that interests so vast and associations so sacred as these can be effaced from Ulster breasts by a political tour of Mr. Chamberlain, or by a screed of riotous poetry from Lord Randolph Churchill.

The points of juncture between Catholic and non-Catholic sentiment are all of honest Irish growth ; the points of divergency are all either the creation of infamous English policy in the past, or the invention of out-of-work English politicians in the present. Even the brand-new and pinchbeck Ulster sentiment which is the latter-day Tory stock-in-trade has no real abiding place in Ulster. The very Irishmen who conceive themselves bound to fight the anti-Irish battle have their own kindly smack of Irishism, which imparts to their most blood-stained declamations against their own countrymen a certain Pickwickian sense. Colonel Saunderson is, at the worst, an amusing man in a dull world ; and nobody who knows Mr. Arthur Johnson of Ballykilbeg at close quarters can doubt that he will be one of the most popular personages in an Irish Parliament in College Green, Orange sashes, Boyne water, insurrectionary rifles, and all. The venom of the Ulster combat comes not from native hearts, but from a bitter-blooded Scotch-

man who left his country for his country's good, and from
a member for West Belfast, whom the dispensation of
nature provided with no more means of understanding Ulster
sentiment than of legislating for the planet Mars after a recent peep at it through a telescope.   The two gross causes of
domestic differences in Ireland—religious inequality and
an incorrigible landlord system—are, one of them utterly
gone, and the other on the fair way to extinction by landlords' as well as tenants' consent.   While this last deadly
quarrel endured, it being a matter of life and death for
the Irish agricultural multitude, Protestant as well as
Catholic, it may be admitted that the war raged with all
the ferocity that words could fly withal.   A generation
ago the discussion was conducted with pellets out of the
mouths of blunderbusses on the one side, and with the hangman's ropes and crowbars and transportations by fever-
ships on the other.   The fierce verbal warfare of the last
twelve years on both sides has saved life, but has not spared
feeling.   It has been a French Revolution, with a good
deal of the lurid rhetoric of the Jacobin clubs, if you will,
but without anything that the wildest partisan could compare with the September massacres or the noyades of
Nantes, through which the landed aristocracy of France
had to wade to a foothold of agrarian reform.   The wounds
created by words, after all, soon heal if they proceed not
from poisonous hearts.   We have had our share of the
wounds, and we are not indisposed to do our share of
the healing.   The sort of language which was a desperate people's only weapon under insufferable wrong and
against apparently resistless forces loses all its justification
in circumstances in which both the wrong is on the high
road to redressal, and the public opinion of the world is
gathering in ever-increasing masses to our support.   From the

outer darkness of Opposition in which the Irish people have lain struggling sombrely for ages, they are about to pass to those Ministerial Benches of a nation which impose their awful responsibilities as well as glorious powers. It becomes us all to cast our gaze forward to the time when it will be the first duty of patriotism, not to combat any portion of our countrymen, but to combine them all. We will have to measure our words. We will have to soften our judgments. We will have to think tenderly of the points in which we differ, and be tenfold more eager to soothe than in the clangour of battle we were ever to strike them. In famous words, we will have to prove that we ' love with all our hearts the whole of Ireland, not merely one of its parties or one of its creeds.' Differences of opinion there are, and will be, and ought to be, in every vigorous and healthy state. Once we are agreed upon the initial principle that all mankind within this island form one heavenly designed national community, in which the will of the majority must prevail ; we can never too often reflect that the will of the majority is not the property of any clique or party, immoveable, unchangeable from age to age, that the will of the majority is a force which varies, which ponders, which responds to the energies, to the arguments of every man or body of men whose action springs from devotion to the common good. While the cause has always remained the same, the particular plans or methods of Irish Nationality have changed according to the circumstances of the hour, to a degree in which no school of Irish thinkers or soldiers—parliamentarians or conspirators—can claim a monopoly of national trust. At one moment, it is O'Connell's words that thrill the nation ; at another, it is Emmet's sword. The United Irishmen began their work with earnest devotion to constitutional reform ; they ended it with an appeal to the Lord of armed hosts.   The Irishman who would claim infallibility for his own particular views of national policy would have to disown Owen Roe O'Neil and Wolfe Tone and Mitchel on the one side, or to outrage the memory of Grattan, and O'Connell, and Butt and Parnell on the other.   The true Irish Nationalist heart has its corner for every man who served Ireland in his day with the best that was in him, whether his glory shone on Senates or on ranks of steel, whether he toiled in the obscurity of dark days or lived to taste the intoxication of success, whether his services to Ireland took the bright forms of literature or song or consisted in filling giant factories with the hum of prospering industry, or in whatever other form, brilliant or lowly, he may have added to the happiness of the gentle-hearted Irish land, or to the golden memories which redeem her sorrow-haunted story among the nations.   In the life of nations, as well as in the life of the individual, human philosophy has never yet found a formula to replace the divinely-inspired words, which stand true of all races to all time, ' Three things remain, Faith, Hope, and Charity ; and the greatest of these is Charity.'   These are the virtues by which alone achievement is possible to a nation : the faith which can see beyond the jealous circle of the critic, the hope which can pass through valleys of darkness with an undimmed spirit of light, the kindliness which is willing to dwell rather on points of agreement than on points of dissent, which recognises that three-fourths of the misunderstandings that divide mankind come, not from knavery, but from human weakness, which has no personal rancour to gratify and regards no true-born Irishman as a foe.   Let us cross in that spirit the mysterious portals of the future that is opening in the colours of a golden dawn before us, and the young men who listen to me to-night can lift their hearts up with the emotions of a victorious host whose eyes have already beheld Caleb's bunch of grapes from the Promised Land, and who will yet live to enter and dwell there, not in angry armour, but in robes of lasting peace.

AN IRISH POOR SCHOLAR [1]

I DOUBT if you would find anywhere outside Ireland a ragged man of learning who is a sovereign in his own right
like ancient Tom Duffy of Lochaun-nyalla.   I am certain
you would not anywhere else find a people who, in mere
homage to erudition, would acknowledge his claim to
lodging, food, and honour, by right divine, wherever he
chooses to turn.   His realm lies among a nest of mountains
dimly visible from the Leenaun coach-road.   For the
tourist shuddering by on his long-distance drive to West-
port, personages like Tom remain, like the Alpine valleys
under his mountain tops, buried in eternal mist.   More is
the pity!   By-and-by somebody will discover that the
snug little green dells which bask by Tom's trout-lake and
respond to the tinkle of his chapel-bell, while the warrior
mountains of Sheafree, Dhuloch, and Bengorm front the
Atlantic storms from their shapely battlements far above,
form a heavenlier place of rest than a good many of the
painted places where the Swiss hotel-keepers are busy with
their arrangements for bands and illuminated waterfalls.
The only thing British rule ever found to do in the glens
under Sheafree was to take away sixty thousand acres of
the glensmen's pastures and bestow them on a Scotch
grazier; likewise to double the rents for the remainder.

[1] Published in the *Speaker*, June 10, 1893.

But that is by the way. If the Sheafree glens are worth
exploring, there was more to be learned of the Irish question from old Tom Duffy, as I found him last Sunday
evening, apostrophising his mountains like an antiquated
spectral genius of the place, than the British public will
learn from three months' debates on the Home Rule Bill.
'Where does he live?' echoed a mountain lad, with
Spanish hair and colour, but an Irish laugh. 'He don't
live anywhere—only wherever he likes.' He had been
at mass, however, and presided over the reading of an
American letter; after which he had 'gone away west.'
We tracked him to a neighbouring farmhouse where he
dined, and proceeded to parts unknown—it was believed
with the intention of 'taking a little of the sun' before
settling his arrangements for the night. We discovered
at last, under shelter of a Druidical boulder, a dark bundle
of rags framing a corpse-like face for which the sun seemed
to have shone its last, and the birds and lambkins to be
expending their music, and the flower-beds of wild cotton
plants and yellow water-lilies their charms in vain. Not
so, however. The old fellow had been ill since I saw him
last, and a film had come over his sight, and his old bones
shrank until there seemed to be a ludicrous excess of
clothes to cover them; but he was no sooner on his legs
and alive to the situation than his frame swelled, and his
stick was brandished, and his eyes flashed out of their
graves as it were, while he declaimed Greek and Latin
verses with the gusto with which he might open bottles
of wine, and demanded to be heard before all the Academies
of Europe in defence of his discovery of the Trisection of
the Obtuse Angle.

A peasant of peasants, and poorest of the poor, there was
yet something in his air and dress which marked him out

for a member of a superior order as unmistakably as if he
wore the hood of a Doctor of Laws. The strands of silver
hair fell into an artistic flourish about his delicately domed
forehead. The withered hand which guided the razor left
grey tufts straggling here and there about the lips and chin ;
there, nevertheless, was the neatness or the pride which
would to the end display the contour of the well-rounded jaw
and the play of the strong mobile mouth. The floss of his tall
hat might have been black in the 'Fifties—for all I know,
in the days of the Reform Bill ; withal it was a dignified
ruin. Its rust was venerable as the lichen of ages on an
ancient monument. Several of the peasants who gathered
to listen to him wore better garments, in the cast-clothes-
dealer's sense of the term ; their homespun finery, however,
carried an indescribable badge of inferiority by the side of his
napless, tawny coat of broadcloth, all but brushed to death.
Strong farmers, who could give a fortune of 50*l.* or even
60*l.* with their daughters, obsequiously addressed him as
' Master ' Duffy—the gracious Latinised title which still
distinguishes men of book-learning in these glens. Master
Duffy looks so old, and so old-fashioned, that there seems
no superficial reason why he should not have seen Grace
O'Malley running for Clew Bay with a prize galleass out of
the Spanish silver fleet ; or, for that matter, why he should
not have seen St. Patrick banishing the reptiles from the
top of the adjacent Reek. It has taken ninety years at the
least to bend his old shoulders. ' What does that matter ? '
he asked indignantly, as soon as he began to rouse his
faculties and shake his stick. ' I was just on my way to
smoke a pipe with an older man than myself, away back—
nil ego contulerim jucundo sanus amico.' The classic words
warmed him like old wine. His head was thrown back,
his eyes afire, his voice rolled vigorously from the chest,

his oak stick partook the enthusiasm, while he burst into whole pages of Horace, and Virgil, and Ovid. It was not in the least a matter of display. It was simply audible soliloquy. It was the delight of learning for learning's sake, such as one dares not hope to find in a lackadaisical modern university. Prosody transfigured him like one of Dr. Faustus' potions. While I was humbly wondering at his Latin quantities, he was off into Greek verse—I think it was one of Thersites' acrid attacks upon the Kings ; and although I could not follow the words, I felt myself for the moment listening to a living Phrygian Mr. T. W. Russell.

But this mood was a short one. Latin, Greek, and Gaelic classics are the luxuries of Master Duffy's voluptuous moments. The business of his life (and this in a mountain-bred Irish peasant is the strangest portion of his history) is physical science and mathematics. It is easy vaguely to imagine how in some dead and gone hedge-school in the mountains, or from the lips of some ancient priest from Louvain or St. Omer, the bright mountain-boy may have imbibed his Latin hexameters. I have failed altogether to trace the origin of his acquisitions in mechanical science ; yet science in Master Duffy's case is, barring religion, the most passionate object of worship of his life. In the days when he was about to be ejected from his father's farm, he travelled to the county town of Castlebar on law business. He there, for the first time in his life, saw a railway engine. The portent so bewitched him that he took a lodging beside the station, and there for three days hovered lovingly about the steam giant, while the engine-driver explained to him its every valve and crank and cog. He lost the farm, but came home for ever rich in dreams of mechanical discovery. In various odd ways he had piled together a little money—as a writer of American letters, as a chiseller upon gravestones, as a pensioner of some tender-hearted priest who marvelled at his learning or found use for him as a Clerk of the Chapel. His only means of expenditure was books—the more recondite the better. With those he bought and those he inherited from some unknown mountain pedant of old, he shut himself up wherever a neighbour offered him shelter ; and there, sternly forbidding even the priest to enter, he carried on mysterious experiments with coils of wire and steam kettles, with results which neither the neighbours nor I am in a position to estimate. One authentic tale of the results of his ingenious speculations is extant. He fashioned a boat out of an enormous block of peat-mould, and invited his mother to set sail with him therein upon the waters of Lochaun-nyalla. The neighbours were astounded by the originality of the invention. The boat would do everything except swim. When half-way across the lake it fell in two, and the inventor and his mother were rescued by a cooled but still admiring public. The weak point about all Master Duffy's enterprises, as in those of most other children of genius, is just this—at the critical moment they will not swim.

But now came upon the scene the Tragic Muse, inseparable from life in Ireland even in those forgotten fastnesses. The tenant of the barn in which the Poor Scholar, with all his books and treasures, had for the moment found refuge, took a farm from which a neighbouring cottier had been evicted. One night of woe the barn was burned to the ground. The universal tradition is that the incendiaries, if they knew that the grabber's three cows were in the barn, had no inkling of the fact that Master Duffy's priceless books and money were there as well. In the morning the cows were gone, and so were the books, and a fifty-pound note for which Master Duffy had a few days

previously exchanged all the savings of his life. ' I
wouldn't grudge the boys the bank-note if it was in a good
cause,' observed Master Duffy ; ' but where will I go again
for my Latin Euclid and the Delphins, I'd like to know ?
I was a gone man from that night—*caput domina venale
sub hasta*—the sport of every ignorant *stroneshuch* on the
mountain.' The *stroneshuchs* were not many, however.
The mountain-men, old and young, who stood around
while the old fellow spouted verse and science, and shook
his stick at Black Care, could not have been more respectful if they had been invited to a Primrose League Demonstration with refreshments to follow. A few charred books
were saved along with some blackened silver coins out of
the ruins, and with these he still continued to hold midnight
consultations, until his sight failed him three months ago.
The charming thing about the welcome that is accorded to
him at every chimney-corner in the Glens is that he is no
longer able to make any return in kind—for the only
gravestone he is likely to be concerned with in the future
is his own, and the boys and girls in troops have learned
to read and write their own American letters as well as
Master Duffy. Nor has he ever condescended to teach. I
am acquainted with another roving Master in the same
district, who comes to a remote mountain village when
farm-work is slack, collects the children of twelve or
fourteen surrounding families into a barn to learn the three
R's, lives for a week apiece with the household of his
different pupils ; after which the children disperse to the
potato-patches, and the schoolmaster departs for pastures
new. But Master Duffy rather looks down upon this
humble trade in sacred knowledge, and has his doubts of
the erudition of the rival master. Whereat the schoolmaster's soul once flared up—' I am a professional gentle-

man, and not a gravestone scribe,' quoth Master the
Second, proudly. ' It's easy to see you are not acquainted
with the Latin tongue, Master G——,' was the lofty retort,
' or you'd know from Juvenal that the man the gods hate
they make a schoolmaster.' [1]

It seems never to have struck either Master Duffy or
his entertainers that he need have any other claim on their
hospitalities than the glory his mere love of knowledge
sheds upon his native glens. He brings the luck of an
ancient Mascotte. He is a last descendant of the endowed
scholars of Eirinn. And, truth to tell, the old man's entertainment would be a cheap price for a verbatim report of
his observations by a winter fireside. I am too ignorant
to measure, and too respectful to laugh at, the wondrous
mechanical discoveries which still steadily shine before
Master Duffy's eye of faith—his Valley of Diamonds, his
Elysian Fields, his Holy Grail. There was an ancient
prophecy that the discoverer of the secret of Perpetual
Motion should be born on the south flank of Cruach-
Phaudrig. Lochaun-nyalla is undoubtedly south of Cruach-
Phaudrig, and the Master was no less indisputably born at
Lochaun. Whatever may be the strict scientific value of
his discovery of a force greater than air, steam, or water,
he entertains a pathetic belief—for all his years and dis-
appointments—that he has only to get a fair hearing in
Dublin to convince the world of the value of his secret.
When the withered old Master wants to live to see the Irish
Parliament that he is told is soon to assemble in Dublin, I
verily believe it is largely with some hope that one of its

[1] On the publication of this article, some kind people sent me sub-
scriptions which are rendering Master Duffy's last days happy ones.
His remark to the Rev. Father MacDermott who conveyed the good
news to him was characteristic. ' Pædagogus iste totaliter extinctus
est,' he cried, with a hearty laugh.

first sittings may be devoted to hearing him on the floor of the House in defence of the eternal truth of his theories of the New Motive Force and the Trisection of the Obtuse Angle.   Alas! even if the House of Lords were to throw down their arms, I doubt whether poor old Tom Duffy's all but extinguished eyes will be there to see 'the appointed day' named in the Bill for the Better Government of Ireland.   Be that as it may, there is refreshment for the human heart in turning from the hideous caricatures of the Irish race painted by controversialists of the Mr. T. W. Russell school to the realities of life in a country which can produce an enthusiasm for learning such as Master Duffy's in its remotest glens, and a population who, through unadulterated respect for genius, provide Master Duffy's old days with a sort of national pension out of their poverty.

THE IRISH AGE OF GOLD [1]

THE Duke of Argyll was at the pains of writing a book to
deride the superstition that there ever was a body cor-
porate worthy of being called an Irish nation. The fun of
the thing is that the Duke is himself a pure Irishman, not
many centuries removed ; and that the history of his own
family is the best confutation of his thesis. His clan to
this day converse in the self-same Irish tongue which their
ancestors brought out of Antrim. The planting of the
Highlands with Irish colonies is an historical fact, as well
ascertained as the landing of the Pilgrim Fathers at
Plymouth Rock. So powerful was the instinct which at-
tached them to their ancestral State, that purely Celtic
Scottish colonies re-transplanted themselves into Ulster,
hundreds of years before King James's plantation ; and
Highland soldiers, led by the Duke's forbears, fought on
the Irish side in all the last great rallies for the re-estab-
lishment of the Brehon institutions. A daughter of the
house of Argyll was married to a rebel O'Donnell ; a son
led the troops of the Isles in the army of O'Neil. For all
his pamphleteering, there is nothing in Inverary Castle
which the Duke prizes so well as the family-tree which
proves him to be the descendant of princes more genuinely
Irish Nationalist than the Prince of Wales is genuinely

[1] Published in the *Speaker*, September 2, 1893.

English. When such a man as he can argue, for the purposes of a Unionist pamphlet, as if it were nonsense to talk of the Ireland of his Grace's ancestors as a country better bound together than the Roman Empire, and gifted with a jurisprudence, literature, and civilisation of its own, how can we wonder if the Cockney journalist imagines that he shows his wit by pulling the beard of King Brian Boruha, and treating Finn MacCoohal on the same historic level as Jack the Giant-Killer?

The part which Ireland took in saving Western civilisation during the break-up of the Latin Empire is recognised by every European historian who is not an Englishman—Thierry, Guizot, all the learned historic excavators of Germany. Irish troops pressed the effeminate Imperial legions in the passes of the Alps. Irish scholars occupied as eminent a place in the court of Charlemagne as Greek scholars in the Italy of the Renaissance. An order of Irish monks went within an ace of dominating Europe upon as large a scale as their supplanters, the Benedictines. The story of the Irish House of Bobbio does not yield in human interest to that of Clairvaux. The defeat which King Brian of the Tributes inflicted upon the Danes in all probability saved England from being overrun by the savage Danish marauders of Dublin, instead of receiving the civilised knights of Normandy for her masters. How many English schoolboys have ever got an inkling of all this? They would blush to be caught knowing nothing of the doings of the Black Prince. They would burst out laughing if informed that the battle of Clontarf was, in the world's drama, a more memorable fight than that of Poictiers; or that Duns Scotus, and Erigena, and Fiachra—after whom the Parisian cabmen name their vehicles; and St. Gall—whose lake is

the delight of Swiss tourists—were all Irishmen, speaking
the same tongue and breathing the same aspirations which
are still to be found among the Bens of Connemara.
Where, indeed, are English boys to learn better unless
they have French enough to dive into the *Revue Celtique*,
or German enough to question Zeuss or Windisch ? They
can easily enough find sound English authorities on the
Vedas, or the Sagas, or the folk-lore of the South Sea
Islands; but they will search the shelves of the British
Museum in vain for any English book which will discover
to them the fact, long familiar to Continental students,
that during three hundred years of the so-called Dark
Ages Ireland was the only country in Europe which
enjoyed culture, good government, and peace.

Irish history is the only department of human knowledge as to which ignorance is not only permissible among
educated people, but is cultivated, obtruded, and gloried
in. The treatment of Ireland is as shameful to English
scholarship as it is to English statesmanship. The statesmen, out of one of the most fertile islands in the seas,
have fashioned one of the most unhappy. The scholars
have either failed to suspect that a literature unsurpassable in its hints as to archaic society was rotting under
their hands, or they have deliberately disfigured the facts.
In an island resounding with Ariel's music they have
heard only the grunt of Caliban.

Still more woeful the tale, the Gaelic race themselves
were cuffed, bribed and befooled into believing their own
rich mother-tongue to be the coarse and lumpish thing its
exterminators figured it. We all know what the French
Terrorists did with the poor little Dauphin. They de-
bauched, coerced, and stupefied the child until he was forced
to give false testimony against his own royal mother. Irish

children, too, came to be flogged every time they were
caught repeating the accents of Esheen, and educated
Irishmen were taught to turn from the history of their
motherland with averted gaze. A great romance might
be written of how the old Gaelic literature was saved from
the persecutions of ages. Bonnie Prince Charlie's adventures amongst the Scottish crags were not a whit more
exciting or more touching in their appeal to gentle hearts.
What a story that of the consecrated Silver Shrine called
the Dhownach Arrigid, from the days when it was borne
in battle before the O'Donels until the day it reached the
Gold Room of the Royal Irish Academy! What more
moving tale of outlaw life was ever told than the story of
many a Gaelic manuscript which is now among the most
precious muniments of European philology—handed down
by some outlawed bishop who fled to France, to some
obscure friar who was hanged in Dublin, and so down
through the Penal Days from one smoky mountain shieling
to another, through the hands of unknown rustic poets,
schoolmasters, and priests, until the day broke, and the
rotting vellum scrolls were found to be as precious human
documents as if they were chapters of Gibbon? There
descended a yellow manuscript volume from unknown
times through generations of a Tipperary peasant family,
half-farmers, half-poets. Its existence came to the knowledge of Edmund Burke. The great Irishman was not a
Gaelic scholar himself, but his Celtic genius enabled him
to divine a Celtic national treasure in its ragged pages.
By his means the manuscript was purchased for a few
pounds. Then came a pathetic discovery. It was written
in a lost tongue. Its ancient law-dialect had been obsolete
for ages. The learned puzzled over its crumbling pages
in vain. The task was given over until there arose four

scholars consumed with a sacred passion for the Gaelic
learning. They dug up old glosses—so many that they
discovered 30,000 Irish words not to be found in a modern
dictionary. They compared, and guessed, and bit by bit
deciphered. The manuscript of the Tipperary cabin turned
out to be the only existing copy of the ' Shanachus Mor '
—that venerable Gaelic law-code which is far and away
the richest European body of laws that is not borrowed from
the Romans ; and the Brehon Law Commission (good
worthy men of whom, I believe, only two understand a
word of Gaelic) have ever since been engaged in purchasing
driblets of translations of the priceless manuscripts which
the MacEgans for generations risked their goods and lives
in order to preserve. The race of the MacEgans, however,
is one which most educated Englishmen are not ashamed
to think of as the enemies of learning and the spawn of
barbarism. They would be greatly amused if they were
told that it was to Irish schools and Irish colonies Anglo-
Saxon England owed the better part of its poetry, its
religion, and its civilisation. They have only to ask any
well-informed German man of letters, nevertheless, to know
that to deny it would be like denying that William the
Bastard won the Battle of Hastings.

From the sixth to the ninth century, speaking roughly,
Ireland was a more compact body of united States than
Britain, Gaul, Germany, Spain, or the Western Empire.
For the one Roman emperor who died in his bed, ten
sovereigns of Ireland lived and throve, and hunted and
feasted, to a hale old age. Her universities of Armagh,
and Lismore, and Mayo-of-the-Saxons (though they were
housed in log-huts, as are three-fourths of the population
of the United States of America at this hour) were as
famous as were those of Paris, or Bologna, or Oxford in

after times.   Her monks gave their names to dioceses as
far south as Sicily and as far eastwards as Lithuania.
She enjoyed more peace at home than ever she has derived
from foreign rulers, from Strongbow down to Mr. Balfour.
She extended her power, her language, her creed over
Highland Scotland, over the Isle of Man, over North-
umberland and Western Wales, sometimes by arms,
mostly by superior learning, piety, and social charm.
Life was simple, pious, healthy, whole-hearted.   Law and
order were enforced with a minuteness that moves the
astonishment of modern lawgivers.   Every parish had its
official house of public entertainment, whose curator was
obliged to keep a fire ever-burning, and a pot full of good
cheer ever-cooking thereon.   The size of an hospital ward,
the bath arrangements, the physician's fees, were all
rigidly dictated.   The law apportioned the support of
shipwrecked mariners carefully amongst the people of the
district who would have any claim for salvage.   The full
university course for doctors of law, poetry, or music
extended over twelve years.   The power exercised by the
Order of Poets, although it led to abuses, was perhaps the
most extraordinary triumph of culture over arms to be
found in the history of the world.   In most other European
countries the Church was the only power that stood
between the brutal barons and the enslaved masses.   In
Ireland barons and even monarchs shrank before the bards
—the Fourth Estate of their day—even as an English
Ministry shrinks from a chorus of condemnation from the
London newspapers.   An Ullave of the Poetic Art, clad
in his white-feathered cloak, was entitled to make the
circuit of Ireland like a monarch, and demand free quarters
for his retinue, his horses, and dogs.   The democratic law-
giver provided that the demand could only be made from

men of the poet's own rank or above it, so that the poor,
at least, had nothing to fear from his exactions.   The
Ullaves of Poetry were the voice of fame, the trumpets of
public opinion, and honour was the breath of life of the
Irish chieftain.   He depended for his chieftainship in the
main upon popular election; for the fittest man of
the tribe, were he a ninth son, might be a candidate for
the throne.   Picture, then, the terrors of a hostile judgment
from a learned versifier, one of whose satirical incantations,
according to the popular legend, could visibly ' raise the
three blisters of disgrace' upon the cheek of his victim.
Loch Derg derives its name from the bloody eyeball which
King Eochy plucked out of his head as the price which an
insolent bard demanded for his performances.   Power so
great of course brought its abuses.   It was probably in
view of such a danger that the law laid down ' purity of
hand, that inflicted no wound; purity of mouth, unstained
by poisonous satire; purity of learning, to which no man
could offer reproach; and purity in the marital relation,'
as the four indispensable conditions of admission to the
Order, and directed that any Ullave who violated these
conditions in any particular should be stripped of half his
income and his dignity.   In process of time, notwithstand-
ing, the learned Doctor degenerated into the scurrilous
balladist.   A national Parliament was summoned for the
expulsion from the country of the libellous crew.   It took
the pleading of the saintly Columbkille to save them.   But
that the saint should have intervened at all on their
behalf shows how much merit, literary and national, must
have still clung to the profession.   Above all, what other
country in the stormy seventh century was so little
harried with domestic or foreign wars that its most serious
anxiety was how to moderate the power of its poets?

L

The other elements of the population were scarcely less worthy of a high state of civilisation. The workers in gold were a more numerous body than they are to-day. The artists who fashioned the Cross of Cong would see no human handiwork so fine if they could visit the Chicago Exhibition. The royal cemeteries along the Boyne are, in their simple way, as kingly as those of Heliopolis. The population of each barony formed one family, who chose their own chief and pastured their lands in common. The first tenancies that began to be formed were rather freer tenancies than those of the nineteenth century, before the Act of 1881 was passed. The people's houses were of precisely the same pattern that the tourist still sees in tens of thousands along the Western seaboard, after seven centuries of English domination. The Church formed a beneficent Third Estate, checking the rich, feeding the poor, investing every portion of the island with consecrated associations, and sending forth over distracted Europe as many gentle saints as Scythia and Germany sent Attilas and Alarics. Civil wars during those centuries were not frequent, and not at all grave. A tribal war meant chiefly the transfer of a cattle-prey from one valley to a neighbouring one. The deaths were principally the deaths of chiefs and knights, who went out to the encounter with the full-blooded appetite with which modern sportsmen hunt lions and tigers, and did not much oftener meet with serious mishaps. The five united States, into which the island was divided, were loosely and pleasantly held together by national feasts, fairs, pilgrimages, genealogies, and (occasional) parliaments. In a general way the strongest of the five kings ruled, and the weak went to the wall. So they did elsewhere; so, unhappily, they do still.

It was the three centuries of invasion by the Danish barbarians that brought all this fair civilisation to ruin and interrupted the natural evolution of the five States into one. No country in Europe resisted the Vikings so effectually as Ireland. No country, consequently, suffered so bitterly from their ravages. Nevertheless, it was only a disastrous accident that prevented Ireland from being consolidated into a united kingdom on the field of Clontarf. Brian was monarch of Ireland that morning—in a far more real sense than any of his contemporaries was monarch of England, or France, or Germany, or Italy, or Spain. He was a man of wisdom and firmness. His son was no less famous as a warrior and statesman. His grandson was singled out by popular enthusiasm for a future more glorious still. All three—father, son, and grandson—fell together on the same day and in the arms of victory. The invasion of Ireland was at an end, but so was its unity as a kingdom. In all Ireland's ill-starred history there is no more pathetic mischance. It might well have been the subject of a national epic, if the eight centuries of unbroken warfare, oppression, and intellectual darkness which followed did not give the Order of Poets its *coup de grâce*. The cause of Irish nationality does not depend upon whether the Ireland of the twelfth century was, what no other country in Europe was, a perfectly homogeneous State, policed like a modern English shire. But at least let us not make fun of the most incontrovertible evidence of its exceptionally good record. I hope Englishmen for the future, at least, will be ashamed not to know something of the glory and tragedy enacted upon the day of Clontarf. By-and-by they may find the story fascinating enough to lead them on to the discovery that even a century and a half after that fearful blow, when Strongbow and his

French knights came to Leinster, the Irish race were still a freer, more civilised and cultured race than their contemporaries of Anglo-Saxon blood, and had again and again all but completed the fabric of national unity, centuries before the King of Paris ruled in Burgundy, or the King of Castille among the minarets of Granada.

THE FUTURE OF THE YOUNG MEN
OF IRELAND [1]

OF all the memories of gloom and regret which weigh
upon the history of Ireland, there is none more tragic
than the reflection that so many generations of young
men should have been born to lives of inevitable misery
and degradation. The blood which supplied their bodily
life, the creed which was the fountain-head of their
spiritual existence, came to them, as it were, under a
congenital curse. It was a crime for them to regard the
gracious green land into which they were born as their
own. It was a crime even to look for happiness beyond
this fleeting world with eyes of faith that did not receive
their laws from England. They were the inheritors of a
country glowing with the elements of happiness—a rich
soil, a benignant climate, all forms of beauteous shape and
colouring in mountain, glen, and sea. But those things
which God fashioned for the people's enjoyment were
turned into the instruments of the people's subjection.
Their country's soft charms only roused the conquerors'
lust. They but reaped the golden harvest for their masters'
granary. The very woods that sheltered them were
offenders against English law, and were cut down and

[1] Presidential address delivered before the Cork National Society,
September 26, 1893.

cast into the fire. The wild animals that provided the
sport of the ruling caste held not their lives on a more
precarious tenure than the tillers of the soil. The agent's
whip cracked, and they paid as he pleased to exact; the
bailiff frowned, and their cabins fell in ruins to the earth.
They came into the world, these fated children of the Gael,
with gifts which might have distanced most modern
nations both in arms and intellect, in feats of body or soul.
They possessed the physical qualities of a more jovial
Sparta, an intellectual hunger which never died even in
the starless midnight of the penal times, and hearts pant-
ing with the most passionate affections, and souls expand-
ing towards ideals of eternal truth and beauty here and
hereafter. But the Gaelic intellect was to be left as
desolate as the Munster plains, upon which the marauders
thought they had left nothing behind but corpses and
ashes. The schoolmaster became an object of even greater
aversion in Dublin Castle than the bard, and was hunted
down with sword and bribe almost as ruthlessly as the
priest. Wherever a young Irishman's eyes turned triple
walls of ascendency overshadowed him; disabilities bound
his arms, choked his voice, searched out his very soul
with bribes and terrors. Parliament, the Universities,
the learned professions, the trade guilds, were not for such
as he. Did the sacred thirst for learning seize upon him?
He must fly to some wild western creek in search of some
outlawed galley that will bear him away to Salamanca or
to St. Omer. Did the soldier's glorious trade allure him?
He must first become a rebel and an exile. Did the sports
of the field stir his hot Irish blood? The lord whom he
outstripped in the hunting-field could have his revenge by
riding off upon his hunter, on payment of a five-pound
note, and could summarily dispose of any protest with the

loaded end of a riding-whip. A more stupid race might
well have accepted the seemingly inevitable, extinguished
every illuminating spark of tradition or knowledge or
faith in their souls, and been content to wallow in swinish
subjection under the park walls of their masters. A more
seductive career might even have glittered before the young
Irishman who had some consciousness of genius, or whose
veins tingled with the intoxication of youth and pleasure.
On the simple condition of forswearing the torn flag and
hunted faith of his fathers, the doors of the University
opened to him, the law laid the property of his father and
his elder brethren at his feet, and primrose paths of riches,
fame, and pleasure beckoned him on through life as
through a fairy garden. Unfortunately, perhaps, for their
material well-being, but to the eternal moral credit of our
race, the vivid Celtic imagination was too strong for con-
tented degradation, and the everlasting Celtic faith and
honour too high-sighted to covet the prosperity which is
basely purchased. The Irish youth of those dark centuries
had an imagination passionately alive to the injustices,
humiliations, diabolical pains and penalties which stung
his naked feet at every step in his tortured life ; but his
eyes never lost sight of the pillar of fire in the night which
told him of hopes beyond the reach of penal laws, and of
powers in whose hands the armies of England were but
the angry puppets of an hour. He chose rather the God
whose altar was the mountain rock, and whose priest
sheltered in the lowly shieling, than the stranger creed
that came to him enthroned in triumphant cathedrals and
flashing with the splendour of corrupting gold. He took
the outlaw's chance, sailed the main, and carried his sword
from foreign camp to camp who, by one apostate word,
might have trampled down his own countrymen as a

general, or plundered them as a tithe-owning bishop, or
decimated them as a Chief Justice.   It is in its way a
consolation for the pall of unbroken gloom which enshrouds
the story of Ireland for the century after the Treaty of
Limerick, that the century did not produce a single distinguished Irish renegade.   It is not too much to say that
our forefathers of that black age in their rags and shame
earned more true glory by their mere resistance to the
voice of the corrupter than the violators of the Treaty of
Limerick won in battle array in all the breadth of the Low
Countries.

Nevertheless, there is a piercing sadness in the thought
how many a hundred thousand young lives, generation
after generation, comely in limb, bright of brain, generous
of heart, born to the vague immensity of Celtic aspirations,
were doomed to sink miserably into the welter of desolation and despair at home, or, far from the green Irish hills
and the fond Irish loved ones, court the dreary fate of the
mercenary swordsman in some uncomprehended foreign
quarrel.   In one century the choicest youth of Ireland
were either shipped to the slave-plantations of Jamaica
and Barbadoes by the thousand, or were reserved for the
scarcely less degraded fate at home of wearing a round
black patch upon their cheeks as the badge of their belong-
ing to the inferior race.   Afterwards, they at least found
the means of dying like soldiers in the armies of the Continent.   The romance which has been woven around the
adventures of the Irish Brigades in the service of France
and Spain and Austria has in some degree lulled us into
forgetfulness of the unutterable pathos of this yearly draft
of the fairest youth of our nation, torn from home and love,
from the broken-hearted mother or the weeping maiden, to
endure the neglects and hardships of the professional free-

shooter, ranged often in bloody strife with their own
countrymen in the ranks of rival continental tyrants, and
destined one day to be huddled into an unknown grave by
stranger hands upon some far-away battle plain.   Ireland
probably lost more of the flower of her manhood in all but
unremembered foreign campaigns under the lilies of France
or the yellow standard of Spain than were slain of Englishmen and Frenchmen put together in all the battles of
Marlborough and King Louis; yet of that rich torrent
of red Irish blood that flowed from the Shannon to the
Danube, there remain no landmarks but some noble Irish
family thrown up by the tide of battle in pathetic isolation,
a French marshal, an Austrian Prime Minister, some tradition in an Alpine monastery, or inscription in a forgotten
graveyard.   Mother and maiden on the Irish shore strained
their eyes in vain for the Donal Dhus that were to return
no more.

In the present century the bountiful commonwealth of
America has given Irish enthusiasm, brawn, and intellect
a more fruitful place of exile than the hungry battlefields
of Turenne and Prince Eugene.   Our countrymen have
not only fought American battles, they have tasted
American freedom ; they have become an imperishable
part of the greatness of the world's greatest State—rulers
among her rulers, pioneers in her progress, partners in the
rich heritage of her giant trades and silver mines and golden
prairies.   They have not only grown with the greatness of the
land of their exile, they have showered countless blessings
back upon the island of their birth.   Even in the glorious
eyes of the republic of their wedlock they have never
forgotten the grey hair and loving accents of the poor old
mother in the mountain hut at home.   The Irish-Americans
and Irish-Australians have achieved two feats for which no

other race can offer a parallel. From their exile they have year by year, practically speaking, contributed more than all the poor-rates and all the subsidies of the Imperial Exchequer, to sustain the poorer half of the Irish population three thousand miles away. That is an unrivalled deed of racial generosity. But they have done a greater thing still. It is their principles, their sympathy, their money, which, without firing a shot, have brought about in Ireland a revolution more potent than many that have been purchased with the horrors of a hundred massacres. The Irish-American servant-girl, who has been so often the scoff of English newspaper contumely, has literally done as much to liberate the country of her childhood as if she were a queen disposing of regiments and ironclads in their embattled might.

But while we bow in gratitude to the great continent which has made millions of Irish emigrants welcome, and has enabled them to bless the land they left in enriching the land they fled to, the mere fact that the first thing Irishmen had to do to benefit themselves or their own country was to quit it, reminds us sadly that emigration at its brightest offers an unnatural career to the enterprising youth of Ireland. And think of all the grisly spectres that haunt the story of the Irish exodus even to the continent of the free. Visit the cholera-pits which make Grosse Ile, near Quebec, one vast Irish grave; stand by the monument near Montreal which tells you that underneath sleep six thousand unknown Irish emigrants who died without a cup of water to soothe their thirst, or a loving Irish priest to whisper a last blessing. Remember the pest-laden emigrant ships that discharged half their burden into the Atlantic depths, and discharged, alas! too large a proportion of the remainder into no less appalling abysses of

poverty and wretchedness and shame in the garrets or
cellars of some swarming city.   Even of those who in more
benign days enjoy an honourable and sufficient livelihood,
for the one Irishman who governs a State, or discovers an
oil-well, or wins a silvern kingdom, how many thousands
there be worn to the bone with the fever, hurry, and
cruelty of the American struggle for life, grinding gloomily
like so many pieces of machinery, trampling and being
trampled in a pitiless material scramble for bread, wealth,
notoriety, with the wholesome air of the Irish hills no
longer invigorating their lungs, and the soft images once
sacredly imprinted on their Irish hearts defaced, perhaps
rubbed away, by the new faith, new interests, new appetites
of a civilisation that sends the weaklings to the wall, and
worships material strength as the decadent Romans worshipped the muscles of the prizefighters.   An Irishman's
natural place, after all, is in Ireland ; and in Ireland, even
in our own day, what had a young Irishman to look forward
to but disability in the schools, decay in the towns, rent-
raising or eviction in the fields, a life of dreary, ignoble,
sodden failure, to close on the deck of an emigrant ship at
the best, in the grip of a periodic famine, or of an apostate
judge and hangman if he dared to dream of being free ?

Why have I dwelt upon the discouragements which
have hitherto depressed the energies and dwarfed the souls
of the young men of Ireland ? It is because these discouragements have in a great measure disappeared.   In climbing
a great mountain we are less apt to think of the Alpine
heights we have overmastered than of the rugged ridge
that still frowns between us and the top.   The melancholy
which centuries of all but unending defeat have bred in
our Irish blood sometimes steals over Irish hearts in the
hour of victory more readily than in the clash of a hopeless

fight.   But the victory of which I would speak to you to-night is not one to be hoped for, or even to be fought for. The victory is here already.   It may and will be added to, but it can never be taken away.   We have only to look around and measure it.   We have seen it with our own eyes.   It has all passed within the experience of almost the youngest person listening to me.   And that immeasurable, irreversible victory is summed up in the fact that the Irish masses from being a horde of helots in their own country have become its masters.   Popular power is still only in its infancy.   But the infant is born.   It is waxing fat and kicking.   It has a life of crescent promise all before it.   Within the recollection of men listening to me whose hair is not yet sown with grey, Nationalists had as little substantial ownership of their own country as slaves have of the golden plates they bear to their master's table. They were a timid minority in town councils.   They crept into the board-rooms of the country unions like uneasy intruders.   They had no electoral franchise except a paving stone or a black bottle on the polling day.   The late Mr. Daniel O'Sullivan was regarded as an astounding phenomenon among Mayors of Cork because he was a Nationalist outspoken and unashamed.   The election of a live rebel like O'Donovan Rossa for Tipperary was regarded as one of the wonders of the world.   Men looked around for a policeman before singing a national song.   Wherever a young Irishman's eyes turned, they met some badge of inferiority, some impassable stronghold of alien ascendency. National treasure went in millions of money to bedeck a Church whose predominance was an ever-burning insult to the Church of five-sixths of the population.   The professions were double-locked monopolies.   The Bar was a forcing-bed of Castle corruption.   Men had to struggle into the medical profession under every disadvantage of deficient university culture. The wealth of the Universities and their mastership were so many bonuses on the production of an educated class hostile by sympathy and interest to the aspirations of their fellow-countrymen. The town tradesman lived unregarded in some foul tenement, his trade shrinking and giving out its life in an ever-deepening litany of despair. The labourer starved half the year without wages, without hope, in a hovel less comfortably appointed than the styes of swine. The farmers all lay at the hazard of an angry word from a flint-hearted agent —perhaps from a rent-warner greedy for his fields. To improve or reclaim meant a heavier burden on his back, to be evicted meant destruction—black, instant, and irretrievable. Whatever was spared by oppression was, once in a generation at least, sure to be mown down by famine.

The earth and the fruit thereof were for the delight of a soulless and countryless minority, who applied themselves to be aliens by profession, and stood haughtily aloof from their brother-men in their barrack-rooms and law courts and high-walled pleasure-grounds. Beyond there lay nothing but the armed power of England, two English parties apparently indissolubly united in the policy of repression, and the dumb masses of a British electorate, uninformed, unsympathetic, and immovable. And if Irishmen dared dream of a remedy, whither were they to turn ? Not to a Parliament where men who bought their way into Irish constituencies sold them on the open market-place of corruption ; not in the wild rush to the arbitrament of the sword, either, glorious though the ambition of perishing amidst the clash of steel rather than of lingering hunger or political corruption. *Nec sat rationis in armis*—for arms there were none ; the might of an overwhelming power encompassed us ; and they who with splendid rashness cast youth and friends and hope into the desperate hazard, lived not to hear the trumpets sound on a green hillside, but to pass through the dock of a Special Commission Court to a penal grave, leaving behind them promoted lawyers, broken-hearted mothers, wives, and sweethearts, and a country soul-sick and benumbed and broken.

If an Irish Nationalist had fallen asleep in 1867, and could waken from his slumber in this year of grace, he would marvel whether the Nationalist majority in Parliament, the Nationalist mayors, the revolutionised Poor-law Boards, the Land Purchase Acts and Labourers Acts, the fallen oligarchy, the friendly police, the Home Rule House of Commons, were not all in a conspiracy to mock him with impossible joys. He would listen to men's converse, and he would find not that they were astounded that the House of Commons should by two hundred several votes reiterate their determination to establish an Irish Parliament, but that the House of Lords should have plucked up courage even for one brief hour in a nation's life to defer the opening ceremony in College Green. He would bethink him of O'Connell, with all his colossal intellect, wearing himself to death in the Repeal struggle without waking an echo in the sympathies of a single British statesman, or breaking even by a handbreadth the adamantine wall of British prejudice ; and he would ask himself, ' What meaneth all this dazing talk of a Cabinet of Home Rulers, of a Parliamentary majority discontented only that the Home Rule Bill is not more drastic, of great English newspapers interpenetrated with the doctrines of Davis, and English multitudes vast as the sands of the sea with whom an ex-Fenian convict, Michael Davitt, is an apostle, a hero, an idol?' He would remember the dreary half-century during which the Irish farmer had agitated in vain even for the smallest viaticum of compensation for disturbance; and lo! the arm of the rent-raiser has fallen paralysed, the godlike pride of the evicter has been brought low, the law that once chased without a pitying proviso the Irish peasant from the soil blubbers out in halting but irrevocable accents the confession that the Irish-born peasant is destined to remain its only lord and owner henceforth, and for all the ages that are to come. Our imaginary sleeper's recollection of an Irish labourer would be of an outcast in rags dwelling in a poisonous hut, wageless and foodless under the tooth of winter; he would go forth to-day through the pleasant fields of Limerick and Tipperary, and, side by side with the decaying mansions of the alien and the absentee, see the bright little cottages of the labourers beginning to light up the picture with their snug gardens, their flowers by the door, and their potato-pits stored to the brim against the wintry hour. Finally, his eyes would light upon the temples of the old faith's second youth rising stately and unfettered, fearing no longer priest-hunter nor brutal law, in friendly neighbourhood with the steeples of the discrowned Establishment; he would find the residue of the Church treasure once lavished upon the persecution of intractable Papists now dedicated to giving the intractable Papists the unconditioned higher education they once craved in vain, and to the rescue of the age-wronged cotters of the wild west from their rocks and bogs; and over all the land has gone forth the decree, which is registered in the inmost shrine of every Irish heart, that bigotry, nor intolerance, nor religious disability shall curse our shores no more, and that whatsoever may be a man's religious faith, it shall be free as the ocean winds and amenable to no censuring eye, save that of Him who made a law for the winds and a way for the sounding storm.

True, nothing is perfected, we are only in the beginning of the daylight, we are listening to the singing of the morning stars. The machinery of the Land Acts is still clogged by a hundred faults and fetters. The Labourers Acts can be annulled wherever the blight of local landlord influence still prevails. Young men are still passing from the schools into the world, and the University educational equality, which the representative of Trinity College itself less than two months ago confessed to be inexorable and inevitable, has not yet shone upon their path. Enemies of the people are still seated in the high places, the emigration wharves are still busy, all the hosts of rank and wealth and domination are gathering for one supreme effort to crush the nascent liberties of our nation under the mailed heel. But it is written as the inalienable charter of our future that whatever is still defective can be amended, whatever we have won can never be taken back. Whereinsoever we may fall short in the future, it will be by failure of tenacity and mutual co-operation on our own part, by some of those little accesses of passion or over-eagerness which are perhaps inseparable from the first transports of freedom in every long-subjected land. But in the main and in the broad, the weapons by which we have won the recognition of Irish Nationality from the Imperial House of Commons are in the hands of the Irish people now and for evermore, untouchable by Coercion Acts, invulnerable to the shot or steel of armed legions ; and by no process that is humanly calculable—not even permanently by any passing folly of our own—can the great reforms achieved within the last fifteen years fail to go on developing and broadening down into a complete apparatus of national self-government such as that for which the genius of Mr. Gladstone has just gained the acceptance of the ancient Commons House of Britain. Grattan had no security for the permanence of his Act of Independence except the elastic word of honour of an English statesman in an hour of emergency, no responsible Ministry, no Parliament that was not stuffed with placemen, no force of public opinion among the Irish masses, no Irish voice of weight or influence of any sort in a hostile English House of Commons except the instinctive chivalry of Burke and Sheridan. We, on the contrary, are armed to the teeth with guarantees for a continuance of the work of liberation that has begun—a franchise which enables the poorest inhabitant of a mud cabin in the most distant glen to raise a voice as potent as that of millionaire or lord in the government of his country and in selecting or displacing Ministries—a public opinion which would smite as with a leprosy the representative of the people who should prove false to the principles of nationality and democracy—an Irish party firmly seated in the inner shrine of the Imperial Parliament, answerable to no whip except the call of the Irish nation, under no obligation to any English party except so far and so long as the Irish cause is indebted to them, and unshakably determined to maintain that independence unspotted, uncompromising, and alert until the satisfaction of Ireland's demand for self-government has been placed beyond the power of duke, aristocrat, or bigot to hinder or to recall—and, finally, outside the circle of Ireland's own strength, a friendly British working population, with grievances and sympathies like our own, a British electorate who make Irish rebels their heroes and Irish Home Rule their slogan-cry at the

M

hustings, a British Prime Minister whose one remaining
object in existence is the establishment of an Irish Legislature, and a British Ministerial majority who have for the
past nine months surrendered every claim to British business in order once for all to ratify the charter of Irish
national autonomy.

There are men who would have us depreciate, ignore,
and even reject all these priceless advantages for our
country; who would throw up allies, Parliamentary weapons,
and progress transcending our wildest hopes, and reduce
the young men of Ireland once more to the bleak alternative
of dreaming of an insurrection which could never come off,
or of flying from a doomed, hunger-bitten, and bloodless
country. I have never given up, and will never give up,
the right of insurrection for the oppressed. But you will
generally find that it is the men who were most ready to
dare the worst when there was no better resource for
Ireland than the grim glory of the Forlorn Hope, who are
also first to embrace the prospect of realising the aspirations of our race by paths of happiness and peace. The
one man who was sentenced to death for the Cork rising of
'67 is as enthusiastic in extending a friendly hand to-day
as he was in pointing a gun in those not ignoble days at
the power of England; and it is not a reproach, but the
richest tribute to the brave men who went out in the
darkness to Ballyknockane to congratulate our people upon
the fact that the Forlorn Hope of that 6th of March has
become the assured certainty of this September night. It
is not an exaggeration to say that young Irishmen who are
in the morning of their lives to-day are facing the future
with advantages immeasurably beyond those of any generation who have trodden this land during many centuries
of its storm-tossed history. They start with liberties un-

dreamt of by their fathers already won, and the indisputable power in their own hands of winning the remainder. If their opportunities are great, still greater are their responsibilities ; for while it is in their power by persistency, energy, and magnanimity to make the future life of Ireland bright with reasonable material happiness and national self-respect, it is no less certain that upon the capacity they develop for earnest work, large-minded toleration, and superiority to all the temptations of petulance or hot-headedness it will depend whether they will bequeath to their children in the coming years a country sick with discord and failure, or a country in which Irishmen will be proud to live and die.

Disraeli's famous apophthegm, 'The history of heroes is the history of youth,' did something to create an extravagant worship of mere adolescence which history does not justify. All the world has heard of Condé, who won the battle of Rocroi at twenty-two ; but if there be heroes to whom humanity is under a deeper obligation than to the heroes of the battle-charge, youth will surely colour with that modesty which is, after all, its sweetest charm, at the recollection that most of the poets, statesmen, scientists, and divines of our own memory—the Mannings and Newmans, the Tennysons and Brownings and Long-fellows, the Carlyles and the Owens and the Darwins—were men whose hair was powdered with the snows of three-quarters of a century, and that at this moment the four-score years of the patriarch have long since been outrun by the two men whose shoulders bear the weight of the two mightiest material and spiritual empires of the world—Mr. Gladstone and Pope Leo XIII. All the same, it is the bright battalions of youth that make a nation's glory or its shame ; it is their faith that dreams,

their enthusiasm that drives, their passion of love and
hope and chivalry that makes the world go round in the
enchanted radiance of the morning, before the shades of
the prison-house begin to close and the illusions vanish,
and the deepening shadows of the autumn evening chill
the blood.

The young men of Ireland start now, not as the disinherited cast into the outward darkness, not as the
slaves bowed with other men's burdens, but as the future
citizens, rulers, and owners of their own delightsome land,
with the inspiring thought that according to the measure
of their own brain and muscle, their own sobriety and
energy and devotion, will be the measure of this storied
island's happiness, riches, and fame in the days to come.
We may not look for a commerce with argosies upon
every sea, nor for a Black Country hideous with blazing
furnaces and mine-shafts—not, perhaps, an altogether un-
mixed misfortune for a race whose breath of life smells
of the country green. But there is a wealth, a comfort, a
field of enterprise and progress within the undoubted
circuit of Ireland's natural capacities sufficient to keep
young hearts glowing and young pulses joyously beating
for generations to come. There is a soil which has never
been suffered to yield one-third of its natural increase, a
surrounding sea, rich with a trade worth millions of
money, within sight of starving cottiers who cannot
gather it ; there are those natural native industries which
the great towns of a thriving agricultural country would
plenteously develop ; there are our river Shannons and
river Barrows to be made the waterways of smiling regions,
instead of being their devastators ; there are the hills to
be again clothed with forests, the unspeakable city slums
to be transformed into workmen's cottages where ' home '

would be a word of beauty to the poorest toiler whose little ones now cower in the darkness and wither out of the sun ; there are the beauties of a hundred unknown mountain glens to be disclosed to the stranger's eye ; there are spreading grassy wastes to be cut up into trim fields, and blue-smoked cottages for the disinherited children of the soil whom the curse of Cromwell drove to the habitations of wild animals and plundered even amidst their rocks.   There is the fame of learning to be re-awakened in an island which gave learning to half Europe ; there are careers to be opened out in music, in painting, in artistic design and invention—in those arts which haunt the Celtic genius as naturally as thrushes quire in an April Irish glen.   Above all, there is the education which touches a nation's permanent happiness more nearly than the learned smatterings of the schools or the attractions of a mere broadcloth life—I mean the learning which teaches a man to love his trade as an artist loves his canvas ; which animates him with the beauty, the dignity, the exhilaration of manual labour well performed ; which leads young Irish men and women to be prouder of the know-ledge of soils and crops, of the dairy and the cookery class, than of the indigestible book-lumber with which they are crammed for intermediate examinations ; in a word, the education which teaches them to look for a living with trained hands and buoyant hearts in their own land ; to realise that here, and not elsewhere, is to be their home ; to appreciate its beauties, its advantages, its associations, at their own very doors, and to find in its clement green bosom the rich elements of a peaceful and happy life, and the pleasant passage to a happier and brighter one.

We have only to eliminate those varying moods of fatalist despondency and hot impetuosity with which centu-

ries of unparalleled oppression and degradation have soured
our healthful blood within. But therein the patient must
needs minister to herself. We have to shake our freemen's
limbs free from the apathy which we were content to
believe clung to us like a settled curse. We have to reject
resolutely the mere cynic temptation—the doubt, the sneer,
the barren criticism which would despoil us of the trustfulness, the faith in human nature, the quality of reverence
and enthusiasm without which our Irish nature would be
as a harp whose strings are torn, a thing of clay from
which the divine flush of soul has fled. We have to place
under the restraints of rational freedom the impulsiveness
which we were free to indulge in the days of irresponsible
subjection. Above all, we have to bear in mind that this
nation comes of many sources and is of many minds, and
that if ever a common interest in the weal of Ireland is to
fuse her angry elements, it must be even as the ways and
thoughts and blood of the early Norman conquerors com-
mingled in the kindly Celtic strain—that is to say, not by
repelling, but by attracting, conciliating, and loving. We
must not conceive of patriotism as the property of any
particular school or method. The methods vary with the
circumstances, even as Hugh O'Neil's modes of action in
1586 differed from his modes of action in 1596, or as Wolfe
Tone, the constitutional agitator of 1792, was the heroic
rebel chief of 1798. Mere methods are accidents, not
principles. The end, the principle, the substance remains
always the same—the emancipation of this ancient, generous
race from the dead hand of a foreign ascendency which
misunderstood, corrupted, and oppressed them.

If it should be given to us to see the triumphal issue of
the age-long conflict, and the furling of the battle-flags, we
hold our liberties but as the heirs, the spiritual partners

of the mighty dead, who with voice or pen or sword still fought the deathless battle in the midnight watches when the camp-fires burned low ; and when our Irish Legislature throws wide its doors, it will be to a nation and not a coterie ; it will be as the temple in which the spirits of the great from all the ages, in gown or iron mail—the O'Neils and O'Donels, the Sarsfields and Mountcashels, the Lucases and Grattans, the Emmets and Lord Edwards, the O'Connells and Smith O'Briens, the Davises and Mitchels, the Butts and Parnells of that long ancestral line will be able to claim oblivion for their blemishes, immortality for their deeds of fame, a kinship and a common monument of glory which moth nor rust shall never dim, whereto with bowed heads and grateful hearts will come every Irishman, no matter what his colour, blood, or idiosyncracies in minor matters may be—no matter even what may have been his faults in forgotten hours—to enjoy the heritage, and ennoble himself with the example of the men to whom it was not granted to hear the trumpet sound over the victorious battlefield.

DATE DUE

MAR 12 '74			
MAY 7 1982			
MAY 5 1982			
NOV 1 1989			
OCT 2 3 1989			
DEC 1 6 1998			
JAN 1 9 1999			
DEC 0 2 1999			
DEC 1 4 1999			
30 505 JOSTEN'S			